POWERLIFTING
1RM Method

Lawrence Farncombe

Grosvenor House
Publishing Limited

This book is published by
Grosvenor House Publishing Ltd
Link House
140 The Broadway, Tolworth, Surrey, Kt6 7Ht.
www.grosvenorhousepublishing.co.uk

A CIP record for this book
is available from the British Library

ISBN 978-1-78623-035-5

Table of Contents

1

About the Author

Coach Farncombe (aka *Strength Coach Farncombe*) has well over two decades of experience in strength training and conditioning. He found his way into the iron game through competing in multiple combative sports and came to love the idea of building the perfect athlete. In this pursuit, he was always drawn to the development of strength and power. In the pursuit of strength development, coach Farncombe himself decided to compete in the sport of powerlifting to better validate his concepts, competing both on a national and international level in unequipped or raw lifting when classic lifting was in its infancy. Coach Farncombe happily admits that the totals achieved by lifters back then in classic raw lifting were nothing compared to the standard set nowadays.

Coach Farncombe's commitment and dedication is well known after two decades of coaching athletes to a world level. He has a considerable reputation as a coach that takes athletes to the next level in whatever sport in which they compete.

His coaching expertise has led him to study and work abroad in several countries, including the United Kingdom, the United States, and Hong Kong. He has a rich history of sharing valuable and often little-known training tips with some of the biggest names in the Iron Game.

Farncombe is an ASCC-Certified Strength & Conditioning Coach, allowing him to work with elite-level athletes in the UK and abroad. Currently, he is the Head Powerlifting Coach for Great Britain and a GBPF Powerlifting Tutor, working with numerous professional athletes in multiple elite-level sports programs.

Coach Farncombe has played an instrumental role in some of Great Britain's best international performances to date, the EPF European and IPF World 2015 & 2016 classic Championships. At the 2015 IPF world powerlifting championships, coach Farncombe's attempt selection protocol helped achieve the highest attempt success rate out of any country in the world with multiple entrants. As any good coach or powerlifter will tell you, attempt selection is fundamental to winning any championship.

One of his many roles as Head Coach for the UK is to identify and select new potential team members for the national team. The primary goal for any coach of this calibre is to assist, train, and maximise the success of the team's powerlifters for international competition. There is a great deal of strategy behind winning medals, acquiring team points, and calculating overall totals when competing in the elite-level of powerlifting, so coaches like Farncombe are usually the ones making the final decisions on all attempt selections. As a result, the powerlifter can spend their physical, mental, and emotional energies focussing on individual performance, while coaches like Farncombe develop the strategies that win the medals.

EPF European championships, juniors' team, men's juniors 1st place, women's juniors 3rd place

2

Preface

This book is a complete guide to achieving a one 1RM when it counts. It provides the reader with an inside view into competition lifting at the highest level in powerlifting. Whether you use the method to help you peak for a major competition or simply want to better prepare yourself or the lifters you coach, this is the book for you.

In other chapters, he provides an in-depth look into the peaking and tapering phases of powerlifting and tremendous insights into some of the lesser known facts on how the sport works at Elite level international championships. He even takes great strides to provide a step-by-step process for performing the fundamentals to achieving a perfect squat bench, and deadlift at the highest level of powerlifting.

The 1RM Method is straight-forward with a strong emphasis on an avoidance of "training to failure". Coach Farncombe references physiological principles throughout the publication to support his training method. He takes the reader through the adaptation, realisation, super compensation, and recovery phases, giving competitive lifters and athletes an abundance of valuable information in order to gain the physical and mental strength necessary to become a true contender in any strength sport.

To get the most from this, read both the quick start and the complete 1RM method before selecting which method best suits your needs. The quick start and complete 1RM repeat in some parts but you will still get a good understanding of the method to achieve the best possible results.

You can then refer back to the quick start as a means of reminding yourself if needed.

A Word from the Author

Writing this book has made it abundantly clear to me, first and foremost, that I am a much better coach than I am a writer, unlike a lot of people that only write books and call themselves coaches. To the talented few who can effortlessly do both, respect and kudos to you. I like to think that I have set out this method in an uncomplicated and easy to follow manner and hope that the reader can use the information, which has taken me many years to gather, to benefit their own training or that of the athletes they coach. Two very simple but important points to remember when peaking for a competition: technique is king, and always train to succeed, not to fail.I hope you enjoy reading this as much as I have enjoyed being able to share this with you and wish you every success in your training or coaching.

3

What the System Will Do for You

The 1RM Method is a training program used by all levels of strength athletes, from novices to elite level. When implemented properly, this training program will boost and peak the individual's voluntary single "maximal effort" on any lift applied. This Book will give you all the tools you need to achieve the ultimate "one repetition maximum" when it counts. The book also discusses the finite details of which you should be aware before attempting your ultimate 1RM.

While this publication focuses mainly on powerlifting, we can also apply the 1RM methodology to improve your maximum strength in nearly any field of competitive sport in which you want to achieve a 1RM. I will even show you how to structure the ideal mesocycle and microcycle for the pre-competition or test day build-up.

The book will provide you with simple mesocycle and microcycle templates, making the entire process very straight forward. I also provide the same attempt selection template that I use with the powerlifting team of Great Britain.

The 1RM Method, as detailed in this publication, also outlines the ideal warm-up strategy and the correct attempt selection protocols for achieving a true 1RM so that the lifter does not over or underestimate the perfect 1RM on the day.

The 1RM Method is ideal for all levels of powerlifters, not just for World Champions, because it is not based on setting arbitrary, incremental percentages based on some hypothetical "average lifter". The 1RM Method bases your new 1RM on previous lifting accomplishments, providing a true 1RM percent that is unique to your individual abilities, needs, and requirements. This is ideal because each powerlifter has different capabilities and different muscle fibre type distribution.

For example, some lifters possess more slow twitch muscle fibre, and for this reason, will always be able to perform more reps at higher percentages of their max effort. So lifters with a higher percentage of slow twitch fibres might perform better at a max 4 Rep or even a max triple attempt. Unfortunately, a lot of other peaking systems out there only require you to perform max triples. Consequently, you are essentially trying to estimate your true 1RM single off of this arbitrary number that will inevitably be higher than what is actually possible. Therefore, you are very likely to miss your second attempt and the critically important third attempt, forever preventing you from building the big total needed to win the competition. By performing a max triples or double you will get all of the accurate feedback you need for the best possible attempt selection without flattening out your central nervous system.

The 1RM method focuses on promoting full neural adaptation from previous phases of training to increase maximal strength when it counts the most.

The Human Body is Amazing when you have the Right Plan!

There is something very primal about knowing that you are the strongest competitor in your weight class, or better pound-for-pound in your division. Now, imagine how you will feel when you are deemed the strongest lifter in your country. It seems that mankind has been fascinated by strength since the dawn of time when prehistoric man boasted of his physical prowess in early cave drawings.

Becoming the strongest you can possibly be requires careful and detailed planning. Whether it is a long-term plan for being able to deadlift the weight of a small car or a short-term plan of peaking and tapering so that you achieve your true 1RM for an upcoming competition; it is all about *having a plan*. But you need to have a *good plan, scrap that, it is all about having a great plan* if you want to be at your strongest when it counts the most and ultimately win medals.

In the simplest terms, any good plan should focus on maximising adaptation from the imposed stresses of cumulative training sessions, while simultaneously factoring in ideal recovery time to allow full adaptation to stimulate super-compensation so an improved level in performance can occur.

When implemented effectively, your body will be in the best possible position to achieve your ultimate 1RM when it counts.

3.1 'Why' and 'How' the 1RM Method Came About in the First Place

In truth, there are many different systems and methods already in existence that focus on improving general strength on any given day.

General strength is not specific and could be moving a heavy object further or being able to perform 5 reps with a heaver weight. You must realise these systems are not specific to improving your 1RM when it counts, and that is why the 1RM method is completely different. It is one of only a few programs specifically designed to create a realisation effect so that your nervous system is primed and capable of performing a competition 1RM.

Lots of systems *increase* maximal strength levels in some capacity and you do not have to follow a single school of thought in order to be successful. You do however, need to know why one system is more appropriate than the other to get the best results for a specific future moment in time.

After successfully coaching several powerlifters in national and international level competitions, I was given the remarkable opportunity to take on the role as Head Powerlifting Coach of Great Britain. While I was holding my first squad session (the squad session is where the UK coaches make final decisions on which lifters to select to represent Great Britain in international championships), I began asking some of the less experienced lifters to outline how they intended to peak for the upcoming championships.

More than a few of the team members had no real system already in place. Needless to say, I was more than a little surprised. Bear in mind that these are some of the most successful, up-and-coming powerlifters in the Great Britain. How could they not have any real idea of how to peak and still be so successful?

This made me realise that all my lifters with a good plan had a significant advantage over many of their more experienced teammates, including perhaps, those who were physically stronger. Even though these powerlifters possessed great physical strength, they often lacked the ability to transfer and realise the strength gains over previous months of training and then display their true 1RM when it counted. They simply could not pull everything together when it counted the most, to achieve a true and accurate 1RM win at championships.

After realising that some of the most talented lifters in the UK were about to compete at World IPF level without having any real strategy or structure in place for peaking effectively, I knew that it was time to share my knowledge by documenting everything in writing.

Just to clarify, if you do not already know about the IPF (International Powerlifting Federation), then let me give you a bit of background. This federation is where the world's most elite powerlifters compete and if my team of lifters was about to represent Great Britain in the biggest and most revered competition in powerlifting, then I wanted them to be fully prepared. Needless to say, if a few of the UK team where not preparing effectively, then what chance did the typical divisional or national level competitive lifter have of being successful? It was at this point that I decided to write the 1RM Method as a Book, knowing that there would be at least a mild interest from the Powerlifting community for this method of peaking and tapering.

4

Why a Lot of Systems Fail
When it comes to Achieving a 1RM when it Counts

I want to be honest, you should beware that in my over twenty years of powerlifting, I have predominately coached unequipped raw lifters. Obviously I also coach and train alongside numerous equipped lifters at the same time, but because I believe that the future of powerlifting is in unequipped raw lifting, I simply have not used the 1RM Method with anywhere near the same amount of equipped lifters. However, the few equipped lifters who use my system always achieve great results.

With this in mind, I always receive very positive feedback from both equipped and unequipped lifters who have used my method. They consistently achieve great peaking results for reaching their true one rep maximum when it counts the most – on a competition day.

The 1RM Method came about many years ago when I discovered that nearly all the top lifters in the UK where performing max triples and max doubles right before a championship. The reasoning behind this was simple. By performing max triples and max doubles, the lifter gets highly accurate feedback regarding their current optimum lifting capability. As a result, the lifter gets a much better idea of what the first and second attempts should be. This is not the case with other methods such as the APRE auto regulated progressive resistance exercise style approach, which is very subjective and seems to be worryingly common when peaking.

APRE or auto regulatory approach to programming, has great value in general prep/specific prep phases, as well as selecting over volume and intensity on assistant and accessory movements in any phase. But many others, myself included, have found it be less than ideal when trying to peak, or get valuable feedback regarding current strength levels on specific lifts in the build-up to an important championship.

Now, the problem with only performing a max triple and max double is that you essentially lack the volume to maintain strength for any significant period of time. So, some of the smarter lifters will use very high volumes in the training phase before the competition to purposefully create a state of overreaching. This way, they hope to super-compensate in the final few weeks and effectively peak at just the right moment for a competition.

4.1 The Four Major Problems with this Approach:

- **Timing Issues.** It is entirely impossible to successfully predict the exact date you will super-compensate using only an overreaching method. Performing max triples and doubles is a successful strategy for attempt selections. However, trying to create a state of overreaching through very high intensities and almost doubling volume in the previous phase of training is nothing more than cherry picking good ideas from other sports. This does not transfer at all well when trying to achieve a 1RM on a specific day. Methodologies that use overreaching as a means of increasing an athletes' performance are ideal for an athlete to peak and maintain performance levels for an entire *season, but they are less than ideal for an athlete hoping to peak for one all-important competition day*. Each athlete recovers and super-compensates at different rates, and the individual timeframe depends on a multitude of factors, including stress levels, proper amounts of sleep, and of course, diet and nutrition. All of these factors are constantly changing and therefore, solely relying on super-compensation as a means of achieving enough volume and peaking on single particular day is far too inaccurate for a competitive powerlifter.

- **Excessive Fatigue in Only Three Movements.** Unlike other sports powerlifting revolves around three specific movement patterns; Squat, Bench and Deadlift, targeting similar high threshold motor units. Excessively increasing volume and intensity will create such high levels of fatigue that most non-enhanced lifters simply cannot recover well enough between the incredibly high training frequency and or hard training sessions. Because the training is so specifically targeted, you are simply unable to recover effectively to achieve an ideal level of SRA stimulus recovery adaptation. Subsequently, your body effectively self-regulates by training at a lower level after only a few sessions. All of the sports that use large levels of overreaching successfully are made up of multiple bio-motor abilities and are not limited to only three movements using only the same energy system and high threshold motor units. By this I mean that nearly all the overreaching approaches rely on increasing your overall training stimuli, comprised of increased skill work, increased strength work, and increased conditioning. When athletes predominately focus on only three movements like Squat, Bench, and Deadlift, which target the same high threshold motor units less than positive results occur. Unfortunately, by following this type of overreaching approach, all you normally achieve is to flatten out the nervous system for extended periods of time and, as a result, reduce your 1RM potential.
- **Inaccurate Feedback:** If you try to overreach before the competition to produce a super-compensation effect, then the feedback about your current maximum strength will be essentially inaccurate. When you are performing those all-important max triple and double predictor attempts, you are also already pre-fatigued from the high intensity and excessive volume from the previous overreaching phase. Therefore, you will never get totally accurate feedback regarding your current strength level or estimated attempt selections. It is important to remember that competing at the highest level, or any level for that matter, is all about correct attempt selections and anything that makes your attempt selections less accurate should be avoided in any peaking phase.
- **The Last few Weeks:** With the overreaching approach, you usually cut the overall volume considerably for the final phase, or the last three weeks. By cutting the volume, these athletes supposedly reap the benefits of overreaching and realisation. This strategy is less than ideal for non-enhanced lifters because the lack of strength training will leave their androgen receptors in a non-anabolic state for an extended period of time. This will create a lowering effect on strength levels and decrease the chances of achieving a new 1RM.

4.2 Different Programs Address Different Issues.

- **Issue #1:** Some training methodologies suggest they offer a system that increases your 1RM, but unfortunately, they also tend to oversimplify the very important realisation phase. In doing so, you generally fall well short of achieving the numbers that you initially thought were possible. These miscalculations often occur because we usually base our maximums on a percentage of our lifting weight during the build-up phase. This is a problem because the rep ranges used during this phase target different motor units to the ones used when attempting an actual 1RM for the championship.
- **Issue #2:** Some athletes need to improve their strength maximums over an entire sports season. In fact, this is the case for most professional and amateur athletes. It is only really powerlifters/weightlifters and a handful of other sports that need to peak performance at one specific moment in the future.

- **Issue #3:** Not everyone is a competitive powerlifter or weightlifter. Most methods for increasing strength were designed for team sports peaking for a season, weekend athletes, or fitness enthusiasts who only want to become stronger in general. Others might only want to show off in front of their buddies at the gym by lifting more weight for 5 or 8 reps. Their strength gains do not need to be publically displayed at a precise moment in time, like when competing at a powerlifting championship.

To put this another way, a training method that improves your 1RM on a specific day simply does not have mass market appeal. Therefore, it will never be a big money-maker for the author. So, no one ever writes one. Yes, I said it! Even though I am taking the time to write and publish this straightforward method, I am willing to bet that I will never get a good financial return on my time and effort. That being said, most of us in the world of strength training and professional coaching are not in it for the money. We just want to share our knowledge and see other athletes improve and win!

Here are some examples of how other training methods can be detrimental to the non-enhanced lifter.

- **Overreaching:** Many of the peaking methods used for enhanced lifters predominantly rely on a overreaching effect. This is only possible because only enhanced lifters can recover from the very high frequency and intensity of cumulative exposure to only one bio-motor ability (strength). Overreaching may work well for non-enhanced athletes competing in other sports that rely on the improvement of multiple bio-motor abilities, such as agility, strength, flexibility and endurance. However, only focusing on overreaching in a sport that solely relies one bio motor ability leads to overexposure that is simply too great for any natural athlete to recover from positively.
- **Insufficient Recovery:** Most non-enhanced lifters simply cannot recover well enough between these incredibly hard training sessions. This leads to inaccurate attempt selection due to large levels of residual fatigue caused from overreaching and your ability to assess appropriate loads will therefore, be negatively affected.
- **Self-Regulation:** This lack of recovery leads the nervous system to essentially self-regulate by lowering the body's ability to train, making it more difficult for the athlete to train at the correct level of volume and intensity to achieve the ideal volume and loads within the final few weeks leading up to the championship.

To be clear, I am not saying that you should never attempt a sensible amount of increased volume and intensity in the previous phase to possibly achieve some overreaching. However, you simply *cannot rely on overreaching* as the only source of volume to carry you through a 2–3 or even 4-week long peaking phase coming into a competition. You certainly do not want to become so pre-fatigued in the final few peaking weeks that *you can't lift for crap!*

4.3 The 1RM Method and the Female Lifter

With the 1RM Method system you will not have to plug your current lifting percentages into some random formula based on one of many different projections. By using these types of calculations, you are essentially only guessing your 1RM anyway.

Each of the many 1RM calculators out there is based on different formulae with considerable variations when it comes to predicting your 1RM. Having successfully coached both male and female lifters for nearly two decades, I have still not seen any formula or calculator specifically designed for women.

This can be problematic because women tend to have very different muscle distribution in their upper bodies compared to their male counter parts and it seems 1RM calculators are specific to male upper body fibre types so are very misleading for women.

Women will normally have considerably different fast twitch and slow twitch muscle fibre ratios, especially in their upper bodies. Therefore, any calculation used on 1RM upper body movements will be highly inaccurate and will obviously lead to less than ideal 1RM attempts for the women who use them.

Keeping this information in mind, all athletes have considerable variations of muscle fibre ratios regardless of their gender. So, you can see that these 1RM formulas are simply much too subjective to successfully predict a 1RM attempt, especially when taking into consideration all the hard work you have to put in over several months or maybe even years.

Now, do not get me wrong. I am not saying all 1RM calculators are rubbish.

- 1RM formulas are a great method to use as a basis for your general training for men, but most do not provide adequate feedback for women, certainly not the bench press.
- Even men should not base their 1RM competition attempts on the predictions of a calculator or formula. This is a recipe for disaster.
- If you want to unlock your true potential, the best 1RM calculator that you will ever find is based on the feedback from your own body as per max effort predictor lifts outlined in the 1RM Method.

Currently in powerlifting, it seems that a lot of methods use your APRE or RPE (Rate of Perceived Exertion) or a percentage of the 1RM from 3–6 months before the competition as a basis for estimating the true 1RM for an upcoming event. All of these methods provide inaccurate feedback that is less than ideal. While they can be useful for GPP or SPP blocks of training, they are still far too subjective for an all-important competition/peaking phase.

With the 1RM Method, you will know precisely what your opener and second attempt should be. The only attempt rightfully left to your discretion on competition day is the third attempt. This is important because a 1RM is a dynamic variable that can change from day to day. Your second attempt should provide you with a good total while giving you all the feedback you need to make the best possible third and final attempt selection on the day of the competition.

Just using your RPE or percentage estimates will shoot you in the foot.

Let's say that you are slow twitch dominant. As a result, you are naturally more likely to be better suited to performing higher rep ranges. Meanwhile, based on your RPE or a 1RM calculator, you will undoubtedly be misled into believing that you can achieve a much higher 1RM than is really possible.

- Unfortunately, these are the very same powerlifters who regularly miss their second or third attempts.
- They usually open way too heavy.
- Their attempt selections are usually way off.
- So, they simply do not achieve the 1RM that they had hoped.

If you are one of these individuals, getting better feedback from performing max triples or doubles is crucial! You need more accurate information to determine your true potential. With better feedback, you can now warm-up more effectively while minimising fatigue and make better attempt selections to help build a better total. Better attempt selection will better potentiate the neuromuscular system to achieve a bigger better 1RM on competition day.

Unfortunately, the opposite can also be true.
For instance, let's say that you are lucky enough to be somewhat *fast twitch dominant*. Your muscle fibre is less oxidative and therefore, will never be able to perform as many reps at a given percentage. At the same time, your RPE will feel a lot harder while performing higher rep ranges compared to someone who is more *slow twitch dominant*.

- If you are one of these fortunate individuals who is very fast *twitch dominant* and base your 1RM on a percentage of your 5RM, then you will wrongly assume that your 1RM is much less than your current capabilities.

- Basically, you will end up shooting yourself in the foot, wishing that you had opened your first attempt heavier. You may also have to take larger increases in loads between attempts due to opening *so* light, based on a percentage your 5RM or even 3RM. By doing this, you will not create a meaningful environment to potentiate your neuromuscular system between attempts. You also risk your total because of the very large increase in loads between attempts while trying to achieve your true 1RM.

- If you are not a competitive powerlifter and are simply testing for your true 1RM, then you will likely end up wishing that you had planned your warm up differently. Wasting energy on multiple sets leading up to your 1RM, which was considerably higher than you had predicted, will mean that by the time you hit your true max, you will be considerably pre-fatigued. The end result is a lowered and inaccurate 1RM.

4.4 Non-Specific Systems for Powerlifting

The problem I have found with many other systems SAID to be powerlifting specific is that they simply are not! Unlike the 1RM Method, most other systems are designed for Olympic lifting and therefore, correctly focus on peaking your *dynamic* effort 1RM. When expressing a dynamic 1RM, the time taken to complete the lift is a critical factor to success, which is obvious because the ultimate goal in achieving an optimum dynamic 1RM is to explosively launch the weight overhead and catch it, which is an expression of power. Whereas displaying a true, non-dynamic 1RM maximal effort lift in powerlifting is not time dependent. You also need to consider that powerlifting has a large eccentric component and weightlifting does not. This makes a big difference when it comes to the training frequency density and the general design principles of the system chosen to peak effectively.

I will be honest with you. The 1RM Method is essentially very straightforward, but like anything worthwhile, the *devil is in the details*. It is in these details where you will discover most of the physical rewards and benefits. I want to give you these details by explaining the scientific principles behind the *why's, how's,* and *when's* of your workout program to achieve the best possible results.

2015 IPF world championships, 105kg junior Thomas Brannick & me screaming

5

Justification for How and Why the 1RM Method Works

5.1 Simple Overview of the System 6 & 4 Week 1RM

Peaking for a 1RM consists of three main components

- **Training Sessions:** Focus on having just the right amount of volume and intensity to disrupt homoeostasis at the proper level.
- **Frequency:** Focus on developing the most effective weekly lifting schedule to allow the right amount of recovery time for maximum adaptation and preparedness to occur between training sessions.
- **Volume:** If you put the first two components together correctly, then you will undoubtedly increase your maximum one rep strength. If you factor-in the right overall volume to offset atrophy occurring, while decreasing enough volume to ultimately peak at the right time and achieve your true 1RM when it counts the most.
- **Specificity:** most importantly the program is specific to the goal, achieving the best possible competition 1RM.

Maximal strength is the Holy Grail for powerlifters. We define the term *maximal strength* as the maximal force that the lifter is capable of producing in the single maximal voluntary contraction, regardless of time taken. Long term improvements in maximal strength are best achieved by performing between 3 and 6 reps with time-under-tension (TUT) of 10–20 seconds on key lifts. This simple formula is what you should be doing for most of the year on key lifts, except when you are starting to peak for a 1RM.

In my opinion, as powerlifters, we are the best at finding new ways to increase maximal strength. In fact, sport scientists and strength coaches of various other sports all look to the competitive world of powerlifting to compare new strategies for increasing maximal strength with older, more traditional methods. They do not like to admit it because the sport of powerlifting does not yet have the same high visibility or generate vast amounts of money as some of the more mainstream sports. But like it or loathe it, powerlifters are the very best at inventing faster and more efficient ways to increase overall strength. The sport of powerlifting is gaining popularity by leaps and bounds. So, maybe very soon, we will finally receive the rightful credit that we so richly deserve.

Recovery, Adaption, and Super-compensation

Focusing on proper recovery time is just as important as focussing on your training program if you want to achieve the best possible performance in a quickly approaching competition! What you see in the elite-level of virtually every sport is athletes and coaches always factoring all stresses into their peaking phase. Elite athletes have different ways of decreasing the sympathetic nervous system post-training while increasing the parasympathetic system on the days leading up to the competition to achieve ideal adaptation and to speed recovery.

- **If you are looking to hit your ultimate 1RM**, then your primary goal should be to promote the parasympathetic nervous system as much as possible post-training through relaxation technique strategies or simply *chilling out*. Quality relaxation is a very important factor for increasing the parasympathetic nervous system as much as possible to promote recovery between sessions.
- **The parasympathetic nervous system** will optimise the following physical systems, all of which have a dramatic effect on overall recovery and adaptation as a result of the training stress applied by the 1RM Method.
  - o Digestion and absorption
  - o Muscle glycogen storage
  - o The proper elevations of circulating anabolic hormones
  - o Protein synthesis
  - o Enhanced enzyme activity, all of which will have a dramatic improvement on recovery and adaptation caused through training stress applied from the 1RM method.

Each training session will disrupt homoeostasis and trigger specific gene expression. In the short-term, this will provide a small improvement in the overall structure and size of muscle ligaments, but the most significant benefits will occur in the functioning of the neuromuscular system.

The improvements from the 4-Week or 6-Week 1RM Method will appear in your intramuscular coordination and therefore better synchronisation of the intermuscular coordination to better handle loads in the ball park of your 1RM.

The program focuses on the optimal ratio between the sympathetic and the parasympathetic nervous systems to promote recovery, or in other words, training days and non-training days. This perfect balance promotes full sensitivity for tissue receptors to benefit from the contribution of the sympathetic nervous system during training to allow you to smash out sessions at full force!

There are several key factors of the 1RM Method that significantly contribute to you achieving the best possible 1RM. One of the most important aspects is the overall balance between stresses caused through training load, recovery, and adaptation, or quite simply, the weekly training frequency. This is not to say that stress through emotional issues or work-related stresses do not play a significant role, because you will also have to take these life-stresses into consideration when determining volume on assistance or accessory exercises.

To the very best of your ability, you should always try to factor in these social stresses as much as those that apply to training. Remember, all stress is relative. Your body does not perceive any difference between the specific stresses of training and non-specific emotional stresses that come from everyday life. Stress in any form has a cost.

For example, if you and your wife have recently welcomed a new child into the world, then you probably suffer from a considerable lack of proper sleep. This extra stress should be accounted for in the execution of the 1RM Method.

The balance between stress and adaptation is ultimately what you are trying to achieve for optimal results in achieving your true 1RM. If there are far too many stresses in your life (emotional, work-related, training stresses, etc.), then you will simply create a state of overtraining and be in a constant state of high arousal from the sympathetic nervous system which prevents full recovery and adaption to training stimuli.

Each of the different microcycles (training weeks) has a significant impact on how much stress you place on your body through training. Both the initial intensification microcycle (predictor lift weeks) and the volume microcycle are carefully planned to stimulate enough stress to disrupt homoeostasis while allowing adaptation to occur positively. Positive adaptation is only possible with the correct recovery period occurring between sessions.

It is important to remember that you always need to respect your recovery days as much as your training days, especially during this peaking phase because you place more emphasis on higher loads, which will be far more taxing to your neuromuscular system than most previous mesocycles. You should also be aware that the recovery process from the higher contributions of the nervous system will take a bit longer than the recovery process from training at lower intensities, which are more taxing on the muscular system.

Factors like sleep, nutrition, and daily stress levels play a large role in both recovery times and the maximum loads that you are capable of handling. Always consider the impact of all of these different variables when planning and factoring in your assistance and accessory work.

Here's another example. Let's say that you are not getting a great deal of sleep or your current diet plan is simply abysmal. Overall, your life is just overly stressed and you are trying to get ready for a competition. All of these stress-related situations that are currently going on in your life must be factored in when scheduling and planning your assistance and accessory exercises for that day, that week, or that cycle.

On more than a few occasions, I have had asked some of my more overly stressed powerlifters to only perform the key lifts outlined in my 1RM Method for extended periods of time. And they still achieved terrific results.

Your training readiness can widely fluctuate on a day-to-day basis because the stress levels that your body can successfully manage are subject to multiple lifestyle factors. If you were to put yourself through a very intense and high volume workout and you drastically disrupt your homeostatic levels, then it could take considerable time for a full recovery to occur. If the training is too tough (for instance, maybe you are grinding out all your lifts), then your neuromuscular system may incur so much fatigue that you simply do not get any real benefits from the training session. This is why it is always best to only achieve the minimum effective dose when peaking.

In a peaking phase, "less is more". Avoid flattening out your nervous system for days or maybe even weeks on end, which is less than ideal when you are trying to achieve your ultimate 1RM.

The principle of the minimum effective dose is very important, especially when it comes to peaking and tapering. Minimum effective dose simply means choosing the right dosage that will produce optimal results and not doing anything more. When this is accomplished successfully, you reduce any cumulative negative effects created by fatigue from workout to workout.

5.2 Stress and the 1RM Method

All good training systems are simply targeted applications of stress, designed to disrupt homoeostasis and elicit a particular physiological response. This system is no different. You need to beware that there will always be both specific stress responses and non-specific stress responses.

The human body does not have the ability to distinguish between the different types of stress that we encounter throughout our daily lives. Regarding the 1RM Method, we will divide these stresses into two different groups – "non-specific stress" and "specific stress".

Specific Stress refers to the physical, mental, and emotional stress of maintaining your overall lifting and fitness program. *Non-specific stress* refers to the anxiety that we encounter throughout the day while outside of the gym. This type can result from family relationships, financial difficulties, work-related issues, getting stuck in traffic, and even raising children. Non-specific stress can also result from certain social situations, such as the stress of traveling to visit the in-laws or even to a powerlifting championship.

Another form of non-specific stress is sleep … or lack of it … during the build-up phase to the competition, which always has a considerable impact on your performance. Meanwhile, specific stress created through your training methods will only be positive if you factor in the other non-specific stress that you are also encountering simultaneously.

For example, let's say that you are under a great deal of specific and non-specific stress coming into a competition. My advice would be to try and factor in the effects of this excess cumulative stress into your training sessions. You might consider dropping some of your assistance and accessory exercises so that your body is still able to positively accommodate the protocols of the 1RM Method.

- A specific stress response would be a specific molecular signalling of IGF or AK1 until protein synthesis and an adaptation response occurs.
- A non-specific stress response would include anything that activates the body's nervous system, immune system, or endocrine system. A non-specific stress response will have an effect on your heart rate, blood pressure, adrenaline, cortisol, glucose, and/or numerous other hormones, regardless of the whether the original stimuli for the stress comes from lifting weights, or some non-specific form of emotional stress. For these reasons, you always have to factor all of your related stress issues into your training phase if you truly want to peak effectively.

I have coached many lifters over the years who perform long hours of shift work in their jobs with very little sleep in between. As their coach, I look at their work hours as just another form of stress. I then factor it into the mesocycle equation. For example, a powerlifter of mine named Graham works a double shift every other week. On the double shift week, he simply drops all the assistance and accessory exercises from his training schedule. He then adds them back into the routine once the single shift weeks return. When you are away from training, you should try to focus on stimulating the parasympathetic nervous system as much as possible. This stimulation will aid recovery and speed up the accommodation while helping you to get the best possible results between training sessions. Some simple ways to do this include hydrotherapy, sitting in a Jacuzzi, or perhaps some morning meditation. If you truly want to be the best at what you do (powerlifting, learning a new language, or perhaps simply being a better parent), then it is just as important to learn to relax as it is to work hard.

Reducing overall training volume is very important during any peaking phase. It is very difficult to account for all of the non-specific stresses in your daily life, including the psychological stress caused by knowing that a competition is quickly approaching. However, you have to give it your best shot if you wish to be successful.

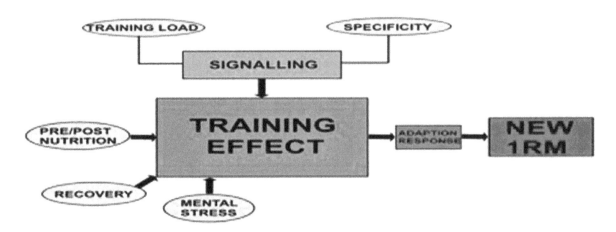

Adaptation to Training model

5.3 Adaptation to Training

When trying to achieve the best possible 1RM you should always consider the overall mechanical stresses created by specific exercises when performing at near maximal loads on your musculature and nervous systems. The combination of the muscle and nervous systems is what we call *the neuromuscular system.*

If you have a better developed nervous system, then you will be able to handle greater loads. This does not necessarily mean that you will recover faster between workouts of very high intensity. In fact, quite the opposite is true. When the size of your load increases, your nervous system needs more time to recover fully.

Even though we combine the muscle and nervous systems together and call them the neuromuscular system, your muscles and your nervous system adapt and recover at very different rates. Muscular systems can normally recover within about 48 hours, but your nervous system will take at least 72-hours or longer to recover between near maximal workouts. Obviously, this is very important when trying to achieve the best possible 1RM and the 1RM Method allows for optimal adaptation due to adequate recovery.

Training with near maximal loads will place a great deal of mechanical stress on the muscles and tendons. In time, this cumulative stress will obviously produce stronger muscles and tendons but what is not so well known, is that training with near maximal loads is also known to create a positive environment for disinhibition of inhibitory signals. To put this very simply, your body will start to reduce or turn down natural danger signals that normally instruct the muscles to shut down and lift less. In doing so, you can lift larger loads, which is another reason that you need to handle larger loads during the peaking phase for a 1RM.

In any training cycle, there needs to be a large enough volume per workout, per microcycle, to disrupt homoeostasis for an adaptation to occur. If all that you have accomplished during the build-up phase to your competition is one or two sets at an estimated 90–95% for a couple of weeks, then there is simply not enough volume to generate any meaningful change or improvement.

Unfortunately, the handful of methods that are currently floating around the powerlifting community, and supposedly promising huge boosts in 1RM, generally consist of protocols with too little volume in the peaking phase to do any good. Most of these methods only allow you to perform two or three sets at near maximal strength throughout the entire short mesocycle. This is simply not enough volume to trigger your body into the adaptation response necessary to convert general maximal strength made in previous phases, to specific maximal strength necessary for a 1RM.

By performing near maximal, high-intensity exercises, you will witness a rapid increase in production of stress hormones. As a result, a large stress response occurs within minutes of beginning your workout as your body attempts to meet the immediate physical demands. This is the called the *intensity stress response*, and it comes into play only if the intensity levels of your workout are high enough to trigger it.

For these reasons, your training loads need to usually be above 85% of your 1RM. The magnitude of the training load placed on the body comes down to both the overall volume and the intensity from each session. Each of these components triggers the intensity stress response while cumulatively signalling the appropriate pathways to increase strength levels throughout the 1RM Method.

The only sessions that you should never miss, if possible, are your max effort sessions. I cannot stress this enough! Always plan ahead for these max effort predictor lift sessions to ensure that nothing stops you from being recovered fully and full of enthusiasm. I always tell my lifters to make sure that they always get to bed early and try their hardest to make their workday as stress-free as possible. I also tell them to stay hydrated and to eat optimally to ensure a great max effort predictor lift attempt or volume session.

In the last few years, I have found Heart Rate Variability (HRV) systems to be the most effective for analysing the body's ability to recover fully between sessions because it factors in all of the cumulative stress, including the specific stress associated with training and the non-specific stress that comes from the athlete's everyday life circumstances.

The Bio-Force HRV System also includes the capabilities to add notes to rate the athletes' quality of sleep. The lifter can therefore, use this system as their overall training log too. If you want to take your training to the next level, then I would recommend using the Bio-Force system to make tracking all these important details easier on yourself and your coach.

For very strong lifters, performing more accessory exercises and less assistance exercises that consist of similar motor patterns to those used in your competitive lifts would be a better choice. As I mentioned earlier, this is because lifting larger loads is more stressful on the nervous system, which then requires more time between sessions to recover fully. To put this more simply, lower load accessory exercises focussing on smaller muscle groups might be a smarter choice to allow for ideal recovery between sessions and to ultimately achieve a peak 1RM when it counts the most.

For novice or intermediate lifters, you will likely benefit most from a slight increase in assistance exercises because your central nervous system will be able to handle the lower loads far better while still allowing optimal recovery between sessions. As a general rule, most women lifters fit into this category.

Let me just clarify something before any females get pissed off at me! It has been shown, time and time again, that women tend to better tolerate higher volumes and frequencies than men!

This is due, in large part, to the comparatively lower levels of relative strength. So, I am only quoting current scientific research while supporting it with my own professional coaching experience over many years of training numerous female lifters.

This ability to handle greater amount of training in a week is a good thing, as slightly more volume in each workout and throughout each week will general yield better gains in strength in both the short and long term.

One thing that I would like to add is that there are some elite level female lifters with such high maximal strength levels in lower body movements that they might benefit from also decreasing the level of assistance exercises just like their male counterparts. However, generally speaking, the smaller and/or lighter lifter will recover faster and more effectively from a greater volume of movements with similar motor patterns, allowing them, ultimately, to peak at a predetermined and precise moment in time.

Directly manipulating the volume of reps between max effort sessions creates an undulating decrease in volume, week by week, ultimately allowing you to increase preparedness to enable a peak at the all-important championship.

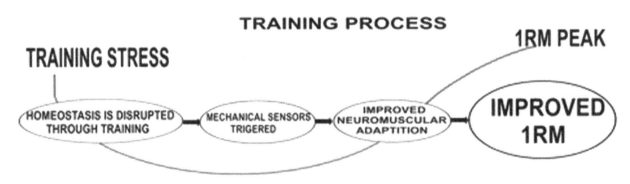

TRAINING PROCESS MODEL

The volume week works as an amplifier, allowing new intensity levels to be locked in; but remember that your goal here is to avoid lifting to complete failure. You do not want to accumulate too much fatigue in your nervous system in the lead up to those very important max effort protector lifts or even worse, the crucial competition yet to come.

Always be aware of your own individuality. All of us lead very different lives, so we always need to take this into account when planning assistance and accessory exercises. *One size does not fit all.* We each have different types of jobs, either manual or sedentary and we all have our own unique genetics, different diets and varying levels of stress. Factor all of these individual life aspects into creating your program to get the best possible results.

During the volume session on squat and bench, the goal is to execute the minimum effective dose prescribed using proper form. Even more importantly, you must avoid *training to complete failure.* If that means cutting a set or reps, then so be it! In my experience, performing high quality sets and reps is one of the most important aspects to achieve an ideal peak.

Due to the decreasing undulating volume that occurs throughout the 1RM Method along with the further taper that occurs from eliminating the dynamic days from the final week, you should generally expect a 2–5% increase of maximal strength above the estimated 1RM based off of your max triples or doubles.

This common increase in maximal strength due to the super-compensation effect means that if you are an experienced lifter it is sometimes worthwhile pushing your estimated 1RM to 2–5% above what you expect to achieve based on your max triple or doubles. However, bear in mind this is only worth the risk in cases where you have a very strong chance of an individual medal or an outright win.

5.4 The SAID Principal & 1RM Method

The Importance of the SAID Principle

SAID stands for "Specific Adaptations to Imposed Demands". It is very common to hear or read claims from other coaches that their preparation strategies are "sport-specific" and will directly correspond to a 1RM for their related sport. However, upon further examination, one will also usually discover that these methods are not overly specific to the task of improving a 1RM. This is due to the fact that a lot of these methods rely on using higher reps or subjective RPE, which as previously mentioned, are less than ideal for a 1RM. Performing max triples and doubles will not only help prepare you psychologically, it also allows for specific adaptation that is as close as possible to the imposed stresses experienced in competition without flattening out your nervous system. Performing volume singles in the last session before the championship allows you to be as specific as possible without excessively creating large levels of neural fatigue.

The final volume single week should be performed under command. Your ultimate goal is to create an environment that is as close to a competitive environment as possible.

It is important that the chosen method to increase your 1RM strives to reinforce optimum neuromuscular efficiency in a specific motor pattern that simultaneously maximises intramuscular and intermuscular coordination. By targeting the same energy system that you will be using in competition (ATP-CP system), you will be training with a similar TUT while allowing for increased motor-unit recruitment, firing rates, and optimal synchronization for adaptation to occur and therefore, allowing you to increase your 1RM.

The term "Specific" in SAID can pertain to biomechanical, metabolic, or psychological adaptations because the 1RM Method employs all of them. It can be SAID (pardon the pun) that the 1RM Method is sport-specific to powerlifting but because of the specific adaptation to imposed demands; the 1RM Method will also have a significant positive effect on your one rep max coming into any sporting championship.

This 1RM Method is specially designed to give powerlifters an ideal frequency per week of training. The individual's intensity load is specific to the athlete and the ideal volume necessary to achieve the best possible 1RM. In other words, simply trust the way you feel.

- **Example #1:** Let's say that you are feeling really strong on a particular max effort predictor lift day. The warm-up is going well, and all the weights feel very comfortable. This might be the time where you could increase the load slightly from that of your originally planned max effort attempt. Remember however, the goal of the 1RM Method is to *train to succeed* rather than *train to fail*.
- **Example #2:** The reverse is also true. On some days you might feel particularly tired during the warm-up. The weights feel very heavy and the workout is going very badly. In these circumstances, there is nothing wrong with lowering estimated load on the max effort predictor lift to ensure that you hit your max triple or max double. This is just your body telling you what you need to hear so you can recover and adapt between sessions.

　　This is an important rule to remember. Even if you hit the numbers at a very big grind, you are still more likely to unwittingly create an environment of excessive fatigue, which could cumulatively increase throughout this realisation phase. Week by week, cumulative fatigue between sessions will jeopardise your body's abilities to recover fully between sessions and negatively affect your body's ability to display your true 1RM on competition day.

- **Example #3:** If you are feeling great on a volume day, then many powerlifters often make the mistake of taking an extra set or worse increasing the load. Remember, respecting the minimum effective dose will always yield better results in any peaking phase. By performing too much volume or intensity you could negatively affect your recovery, which is going to be so very important on that next important max effort day…or worse…the day of competition!

In general, you should never be feeling overly tired when performing the 1RM Method.
It is always best to first drop some of the assistance and accessory exercises if you are feeling overly tired.

Adequate recovery periods between sessions is crucial. The 1RM Method respects the significance of the minimum effective dose necessary for achieving vast improvements in strength training. If you are feeling fatigued due to your training schedule or other external factors, then consider dropping a set on the volume days. After all, you should not be grinding out set after set. These sets should always be tough to perform, while still consisting of clean, technically-sound reps. The only set that might be a bit of a grind would be your last full set of the day.

There are only a few different peaking methods out there and they are nearly all based on a 1RM training percentage that you performed several months prior. These methods are obviously highly inaccurate and certainly not ideal for a competition. Remember, your 1RM is a dynamic variable that changes from day to day and even more so from month to month. So even though these methods might seem worthwhile for determining a 1RM *range* in the months preceding a competition, they are far too subjective when you are peaking for a championship.

After numerous discussions with other head coaches from all over the world, I clearly see a pattern. When heading into competitions, nearly all of the most informed powerlifting coaches base their athletes' 1RM attempts for competition day on max triples or doubles performed within a few weeks before the competition. You can use this inside information to your advantage.

You should also be aware that many of the other strength training systems are designed *by* enhanced lifters *for* enhanced lifters. Therefore, the included information and methodologies of these other systems do not necessarily transfer particularly well to *non-enhanced lifters*.

Remember, you can use the 1RM Method for improving *any* individual 1RM on *any* lift. You do not have to be a competitive powerlifter to reap the benefits of this system. You could be an athlete preparing for a battery of tests, an athlete aiming optimise the ability to perform a 1RM on a different lift specific to your sport, or you could simply be using the 1RM Method to improve and peak your maximal strength level before going back to a higher-volume, lower-intensity training system. What I am trying to highlight is that the 1RM Method does not have to be used solely for powerlifting. Do however, be aware that it is originally designed for powerlifting and not for anything else such as the Olympic style of weightlifting, like so many other methods are.

The goal of the 1RM Method is to:

- *Reduce fatigue*
- *Elevate fitness*
- *Enhance specificity*

1. **Reduce fatigue as much as possible**: Volume, rather than intensity is the main contributor to fatigue. In the 1RM Method, we focus on an overall undulating decrease in volume and training frequency density in the last microcycle to allow for super-compensation and peaking to take place.
2. **Elevate fitness/preparedness as high as possible:** Reducing fatigue is paramount if we are to elevate fitness/preparedness, or in our case, increase maximal strength and create a peaking effect when it counts

the most, for a competition. The trick is to avoid bringing the volume down so fast that we lose our overall level of fitness. Strength can be maintained and even increased for short periods of time through much lower volume levels than is needed to build maximum strength in the first place. On this basis, the 1RM Method systematically reduces the overall volume, allowing fatigue to be minimised so that your maximal strength levels are subsequently displayed in their entirety.

3. **Enhance specificity:** Performing max triple and max double testing results in the following…

   o You will be much better prepared to more closely estimate your ideal attempt selections for the day of competition.

   o You will have a much better idea of the correct warm-up that will allow you to display a true 1RM during the event.

   o You will be better prepared physiologically and better able handle the psychological stress associated with max effort attempts during a competition.

   o Finally, performing volume singles at a meaningful load under command in the last week of the 1RM Method, you achieve the best possible specificity without actually attempting a 1RM, which could potentially create so much neural fatigue that it may take weeks to recover.

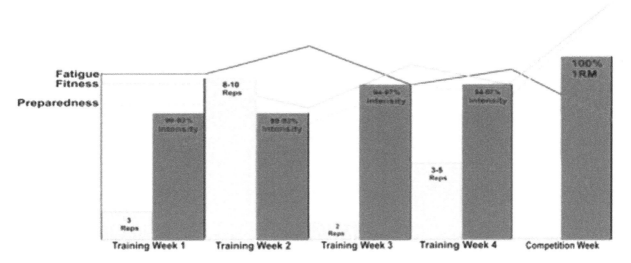

FITNESS FATIGUE PREPAREDNESS MODEL

The 1RM Method focuses on three main points:

1. **The 1RM Method stimulates just the right *amount/volume* of overall neural stress needed to trigger the body to adapt and respond efficiently.**

2. **The 1RM Method focuses on the right *load/intensity to create the right level of* neuromuscular stress necessary for positive neural adaptation to occur, leading to the desired realisation of maximal strength.**

3. **The 1RM Method provides the needed uniform decreases in overall volume that results in the body's ability to super-compensate and peak at the appropriate and precise day of your competition.**

Factored into the 1RM Method is the allowance for sufficient recovery time between sessions for ideal adaptation to occur. As a result, you should be very careful not to overindulge on the supra-maximal assistance exercises during the peaking phase, boards/bands/chains/partials being an example.

5.5 Before Beginning the 1RM Method.

Take into consideration the following factors:

- **Health Issues:** Always consult your doctor before beginning any training method, including the 1RM Method. Always inform the physician of any pre-existing health problems.
- **Age**: Your age will affect how fast you recover from each session.
- **Training Age**: How long have you been performing resistance training?
- **Muscular Profile:** Generally, those with greater amounts of fast twitch muscle fibres will require longer recovery periods between sessions. The opposite is true for slow twitch lifters.
- **Psychological Profile:** If you are a stress-head, then it will take longer to recover fully because all stress is relative. The opposite is true for individuals who tend to be more *chilled out*.
- **Dietary Habits**: If you have a very poor diet, then it takes longer to recover fully. Also, your adaptation to training stimuli will be less than optimal. Again, the opposite is true if you have a healthy diet.
- **Injuries:** I do not think that we have to explain this one.

6

Basic Overview of the 1RM Method

It should be noted that the 1RM method incorporates the use of dynamic effort on sport specific movements for numerous reasons. Firstly, to get more time under the bar, train in or maintain an ideal motor pattern while not incurring high levels of neural fatigue created by maximal loads. Secondly, dynamic effort method lifting also works as active recovery between maximum effort sessions for better fatigue management. I have found there to be a definite correlation between performing dynamic work and the nervous system's ability to better recover between sessions in phase focusing on maximum loads being lifted. I am the first to admit dynamic method effort lifting alone is not going to make you incredibly strong and achieve new PBs. I use dynamic effort loads with this peaking phase as I have found that it better potentiates sequential maximal effort lifting. As many of us are aware, lifting maximum effort loads can make you feel very sluggish due to high levels of neural fatigue.

I have found over many years performing dynamic effort work in conjunction with maximum effort loads of above 87%, that the dynamic work performed has a priming up effect on the nervous system between max effort sessions. But I'll let the sports scientists debate the how's and whys of that one.

One of the most important aspects of the 1RM Method is in successfully managing the very high levels of psychological stress that come from performing such highly intensive max triples and doubles during the build-up phase for the competition. Successfully managing these high stress levels will prepare you for the day of the competition when your mind set needs to be 110% focused on achieving your optimum 1RM at a single moment in time.

Other strength training systems that do not allow you to experience this extreme level of anxiety will be far less specific in their implementation strategies. These systems tend to leave you guessing as to whether you will have the right mental attitude on day of the competition to really pull it off!

Throughout my 1RM Method, you will get consistent and accurate feedback, which allows you to make the most appropriate attempt selections possible. Believe me when I tell you that physically testing your max triple and max double is a far better strategy than subjecting yourself to some random number spat out by a 1RM Calculator, or some subjective RPE. In reality, these calculations are nothing more than an extremely poor estimation. It is not a true indication of what you are truly capable of on the day of the competition.

By incorporating the 1RM Method along with the attempt selection template while performing max doubles and triples, you take the guesswork out of determining the real-life maximum loads that you are truly capable of handling.

The 1RM Method is like walking a tightrope of specificity. It targets the same mechanics and predominantly recruits the same muscle fibre type while creating important psychological pressure to achieve PB maximums during every other max effort predictor lift training session.

The 1RM Method is entirely focused on finding that exact maximum lifting weight that you can successfully hit at a precise future moment in time – competition day! However, my system does not require you to perform subjective guesswork based on only one session of max triples and doubles during the build-up phase.

Instead, the 1RM Method gives you all the positive and accurate feedback that you need to make the best possible attempt selections for your competition. It takes into consideration the most important aspect of achieving a 1RM on any given day. A 1RM is a dynamic variable that changes from day to day based on multiple factors like training stress, social stress, quality of sleep, recovery periods, nutrition, and overall preparedness. The 1RM Method gives you the best possible feedback and therefore, the best possible chance of getting it right on the money when it counts the most!

MON	TUE	WED	THU	FRI	SAT	SUN
1x3 Max Triple squat, 1x3 max triple deadlift assistant & accessory	Dynamic Bench Assistant & accessory work		Dynamic Squat Assistant & accessory work	1x3 Max Triple bench Assistant & accessory work		
5x2 Volume doubles squat 5x2 deadlift triples 80%, Assistant & accessory	Dynamic Bench Assistant & accessory		Dynamic Squat Assistant & accessory work	5x2 Volume double bench Assistant & accessory work		
1x2 Max Double squat 1x2 max double deadlift Assistant & accessory	Dynamic Bench Assistant & accessory work		Dynamic Squat Assistant & accessory work	1x2 Max double bench Assistant & accessory work		
5x1 Volume singles squats 4x2 deadlift doubles at 85%	5x1 volume singles bench Assistant & accessory work					Meet

4 Week 1RM method example

This is the system you should use if you have been training at 85% or more of your estimated 1RM on the key lifts and performing both squats and deadlifts in the same training session.

How the 1RM Method works with the nervous system to achieve the ideal adaptation for increased 1RM strength.

Week One

Performing a max triple protector lift, remember this should be a good quality triple where only the last rep might be a grind. Your triple will normally be roughly between 90–94% of your 1RM, but do not worry too much about the estimated percentage as the weight you lift is far more important. By only performing one quality set you will not incur excessive neural fatigue, but will still reap the benefits of ideal morphological and neurological recovery from previous training.

Week Two

Reduce your reps by one and perform 5 sets of doubles. Your goal is to achieve 10 Reps total volume with a minimum volume threshold of 8 reps. I cannot stress enough the importance of not grinding out reps on the max triple predictor lift in week one. Grinding out reps on your max effort predictor lifts will likely mean you will be using a percentage of your estimated 1RM which will be too high to achieve the ideal volume for positive adaption to occur. By performing only one quality set, you will not incur excessive neural fatigue.

The increase in volume in week two will offset any loss of strength caused by potential muscle atrophy.

If you are respecting the golden rule of not *grinding out the predictor lift, you should not be* struggling before, at least, set 3. If you do start to struggle by set 3, simply perform two sets of singles, achieving 8 reps in total. This can be considered the minimum effect dose for positive adaption to occur.

If, for whatever reason, you have respected the golden of not excessively grinding out on the single set max triples but you are still struggling to achieve the recommend volume, chances are you are getting sick or have way too much non-specific stress going on in your life and your body is telling you not to do so much. If this is the case, listen to it and rest.

Week Three

Perform a good quality max double protector lift, which will generally be between 94 -97% of your 1RM. Again, do not worry too much about the estimated percentage as the weight you lift is far more important. The max double performed in week three is a great gauge of what your second attempt should be at the upcoming championship. By only performing one quality set, very little excessive neural fatigue will occur.

Week Four

Reduce your reps by 1 and perform 5 sets of singles. Your goal here is to achieve 5 reps total, with a minimum volume threshold of 3 singles. This is why it is so important not to grind out reps on the max double predictor lift in week 3. Grinding out reps on your max effort predictor lifts will likely mean you will be using a percentage of your estimated 1RM that is too high to achieve the ideal volume for positive adaption to occur. The increase in volume in this final week will offset any chance of potential muscle atrophy occurring with loss of strength before the big day.

It may be tough, but you should not be grinding and struggling before set 3 as long as you have respected the golden rule of not grinding out the predictor lift the week before. However, if you do struggle by set 3, this could mean you are getting sick or have way too much non-specific stress in your life and your body is telling you to slow down. Again, if this is the case, listen to it, call it a day and save your energy for the championship.

I want to reiterate that the volume week will offset any potential for muscle atrophy over this competition mesocycle, while allowing the nervous system enough recovery between max effort lifts. Your nervous system will fully super-compensate during the full few recovery days before the competition event. When we implement this system properly, powerlifters and other athletes can successfully achieve the ultimate one rep maximum on the precise day of the competition.

Okay. So why not just dumb it down and keep it simple like virtually every other powerlifting system already out there today? Why not just say, "To peak for the best possible 1RM, just perform between 92- 97% of your 1RM maxes for only two weeks"?
Sure, I suppose we could "dumb it down", but that would be incredibly, well, dumb! The simple answer is that you will never achieve full realization in just two short weeks. You will stand a better chance in 3 weeks, but in my experience, 4 weeks is perfect if you have been training with 85% or more in your previous training phase.

Here is a good example of why two weeks is not enough time.

- **Example:** Let's say that you start a new training system that requires you to perform a basic 5x5 protocol (five sets of five reps). Even though we all know that the 5x5 protocol is a great training system for all levels of lifters that targets between 80–85% of your 1RM, the *first week* of the system will nearly kill you! *By Week 2*, it becomes only marginally easier, but it is still excruciating. *In Week 3,* the workout is still extremely demanding, both physically and mentally. It is only *in Week 4* that the 5x5 protocol begins to appear even slightly manageable. That's because it takes most lifters a minimum of four exposures to similar training stimuli to achieve the full transmutation/realization effect. The reason many peaking methods are over simplistic is because after 2 weeks of much lower volume and increased intensity, your preparedness and fitness suffers and your strength starts to decrease because of the low volume of training necessary to peak the nervous system.

Remember, a *MINIMUM* of four exposures to similar training stimuli is essential. This guideline is especially true for powerlifters training within the 85% 1RM range for the pervious phase before the build-up for a competition event.

(The 1RM Method is simply a linear step loading model that undulates decreasing volume, thereby allowing a super-compensation effect to occur. This method is a form of concurrent training predominantly focussing maximal strength realisation while supporting muscle hypertrophy & power.)
The 1RM

With the 1RM Method, volume and intensity vary inversely and the volume decreases gradually over the course of training, allowing super-compensation to be achieved at the correct time.

The 1RM Method is structured to maximise specific mechanical stresses that signal the body to increase protein synthesis on volume microcycles.

- If you are coming to the 1RM Method directly from a HIHF method, or any method that has you training under 85% of your 1RM, then the 6-Week 1RM Method really acts as both a transmutation and realization model, allowing you to peak for your ultimate 1RM performance.
- If your previous training mesocycle consists of performing over 85% of your 1RM or above, then the 4-Week 1RM Method will act as a realization phase, allowing you to peak for your ultimate 1RM performance, but in a shorter time frame.
- The 1RM Method uses both psychological and physiological preparation techniques and therefore, truly allows you to perform at your best when it counts the most, at a competition.
- The 1RM Method adheres to the SAID principles (Specific Adaptation to Imposed Demands).
- The 1RM Method is designed to avoid possible onsets of critical levels of fatigue and overtraining by undulating the volume in each microcycle week.
- The 1RM Method facilitates each microcycle through the potentiation of the previous microcycle.
- The 1RM Method also heavily stimulates the nervous system when performing single set max effort predictor lift microcycles.
- The 1RM Method also allows enough time for the nervous system to recover fully for positive adaptation to occur during volume microcycles.
- The 1RM Method then counteracts premature strength loss, which is normally a consequence of having to considerably decrease the volume because of an increase in intensity.

In very basic terms, the volume microcycles create just enough physiological stress to maintain and even increase muscle hypertrophy, thereby offsetting any chance of premature loss in strength due to reduced volume to accommodate increasing intensity. Each microcycle stimulates the potentiation of the body for the next microcycle, all of which leads to maximal 1RM performance on a specific day that you need it the most!

You do not want to miss your attempts. If you do, then you will not have any precise loads to base the following weeks training on. Remember, performing quality reps under 20-seconds each will target the high threshold motor units responsible for achieving a huge 1RM.

The first week of the 1RM Method is the most important to get right!

While executing your max effort attempts, you might consider grinding out the last rep a little. However, *never* grind out on the very first rep. If you make this mistake, immediately STOP, rack the bar, and then simply drop the weight slightly to a level that you honestly believe you can achieve. Rest for a minimum of 6-minutes and then go for a more sensible number. In my experience you will only have one second chance or your nervous system will take too big a hit, so do not mess it up.

If you happen to fail on your last rep in the max four, triple, or double (which can sometimes happen), then avoid dropping the weight at all costs. Your nervous system will likely be stressed to such a degree that going for another attempt is pointless. Simply subtract 2.5% off of your attempt and use this new number when executing the volume microcycle the following week.

- An example in KG: If you are attempting 220KG for a max triple and miss your last rep, then subtract 2.5% of the attempt = 214.4KG. Even better, round it up to 215KG. This is what you will use to perform the volume doubles in the next microcycle.
- An example in Lbs: If you are attempting 485 lbs for a max double and miss your last rep, then subtract 2.5% of the attempt = 473 lbs. Round it up to 475 lbs. This is what you will use to perform the volume singles in the final week before the competition.

I can't state this enough! You should never miss more than one rep on the max four, triple, or double!

If you happen to miss more than one rep, then you are doing something very wrong. You likely have not implemented the 1RM Method properly or perhaps did not prepare well enough during the few days leading up to your session. Another possibility is that you are getting sick for whatever reason, so go home! Rest up! All you can do is try to plan better for your next max effort predictor lift. I will expand far more in later chapters, but you will have to use an estimate based on your training load or a load you have achieved previously to work out what your max four or triple should be. You will need this to plan the load that you should use in the volume week. Remember, it is always better to slightly under estimate the load and perform high quality triples or doubles in the volume week. If you miss both of your reps on the max double predictor lift, then you have likely not prepared well once again. You can regroup during the final volume single session by performing five sets of singles at your estimated 95–97%.

The concept of how the 1RM Method works in a physiological sense is pretty straightforward. This system helps offset undesirable levels of stress caused by standard linear progression overload systems by step loading the intensity while decreasing the undulating volume throughout the entire method to increase preparedness.

For instance, when performing a true max effort predictor lift session, you will be performing considerably less volume even with a slightly longer warm-up as suggested. The goal is to create considerable neurological stress with the true max effort attempt to allow you to tap into high-threshold motor units that will be recruited when performing your true 1RM. By only performing one set of true max effort loads, there is less neuro-muscular stress, allowing positive adaptation to occur and speeding up recovery.

The problem with "one-set-to-failure" is that there are not enough exposures to stimuli to cause any lasting adaptation, especially over a few weeks.

This is another reason why simply doing a max triple one week and then a max double the next does not ideally prime the nervous system to perform a true 1RM. This is where planning-in microcycles with high volumes is a very important part of the 1RM Method. The high volume effectively cements-in training intensity, allowing the neuromuscular system to handle increased loads most effectively.

The decreasing undulating volume and linear step loading intensity allows both the musculoskeletal system and the nervous systems to recover fully between training sessions and improve adaptations simultaneously, effectively boosting your 1RM.

Now, by cyclically undulating volume between planned microcycles, you reap the benefits of a speedier recovery while also allowing for super-compensation, which ultimately leads to superior physical adaptation and a significantly improved 1RM.

Also regarding volume microcycles, you will not just be creating the ability of the body to handle new loads. You are also essentially becoming accustomed to handling large loads for multiple sets, offsetting any muscle atrophy that can be a by-product of other peaking systems that drastically reduce volume to accommodate an increase in intensity.

Another important aspect that the 1RM Method offers is purely psychological. Lifters will grow accustomed to getting *psyched up* to hit their all-important max lifts like triples and doubles. Then in the final week when performing your volume singles, you should execute these singles under commands and as much as possible, in a competition setting. This will help you fully prepare, psychologically, for what you are about to do in 4–7 days' time.

The 1RM Method utilises high-intensity protocols, which allows you to maximise the neuromuscular system for a 1RM. It was never meant to be used all the time or outside of the peaking phase before a competition. I have had great success using this system back–to-back, or in other words, building up to one championship and then building up to another championship immediately afterwards.

Personally, I have never had any lifter perform a lower 1RM when implementing the 1RM Method in consecutive competitions. On a few occasions, I have even witnessed another increase in 1RM during the second competition. I am a great believer in performing assistance and accessory exercises to target intrinsic and extrinsic strength deficits as a means of offsetting strength plateaus and reducing the chances of injury. As a result, I generally only recommend performing the 1RM Method once, that way you can focus on training out any imbalances and experience the best possible long-term progression.

Never try to run the 1RM Method three consecutive times. In my experience, the nervous system starts to get flat and you will start feeling very beat up and unmotivated to hit good numbers.

A word of caution: I have tried running this peaking program for three consecutive times in the past *and it has always produced* minimal results at best on the third time round. I have only used this approach when my lifters were competing in multiple consecutive or simultaneous compulsory qualification competitions or national championships.

It is unlikely that you will ever need to peak for your 1RM for three consecutive competitions, but if you ever do, I would always recommend picking the two most important championships for the 1RM Method. Then simply train through the least important competition and perform some comfortable 90–94% lifts.

- **Important Fact #1: Avoid excessive grinding!**
  It is critical that your max 4RM, max 3RM, and max 2RM are not technically bad grinders! You want these max effort sessions to consist of excellent technical form. At the very worst, your last rep can be a bit of a grind but still technically sound. And this is only for your very last rep on predictor lifts. If your first rep is a grind, rack it and go with your previous load as your max triple or double. This is why it is important to not take too big a jump between attempts. It is very important to respect this protocol! You do not want to leave it in the gym. Further information on exact percentages and attempt selection can be found in the complete 1RM chapter.
- **Important Fact #2: Watch out for fatigue!**
  If you are grinding out nearly every session, then by the time you get to the competition your neuromuscular system will be almost completely flat. As a result, you will be far too tired and too unmotivated to compete successfully for the win!
- **Important Fact #3: Pay attention to volume!**
  The 1RM Method undulates volume, which not only aids recovery but also helps cement-in new levels of neuromuscular strength. The volume acts as a fixer for the intensity and maximises adaptation through decreasing undulating volume while progressively increasing overload.
- **Important Fact #4: Focus on the true goal!**
  The whole point of the 1RM Method is to attain the best possible 1RM by the time of the competition. Do not lose sight of this all-important goal throughout the program!

- **Important Fact #5: Attempt selection for warm-ups!**
  It is important you do not to take too big a jump between attempts on the max effort predictor sessions. You will achieve slightly more volume by performing medium to small increases in load between attempts. Once you are at about 80% of your estimated max effort triple or double predictor lift, a 5% increase in weight between attempts is the way to go. This way, if you miss your last attempt you can simply go with the previous attempt as your predictor lift.

- **Important Fact #6: Musculature coronation is key!**
  Improvements in strength that come from executing the 1RM Method will be largely due to the better intra- and inter-musculature coronation.

- **Important Fact #7: Technique, Technique, Technique!**
  I can't state this point enough! Remember that your max 4RM, max 3RM, and max 2RM, should not be sloppy grinders. You will be training at too high a percentage for anything positive to carry over from grinding out lifts. So you want to perform all key lifts with good, solid technique. You can grind out your last rep, but you should definitely not grind out any of your the others. If you ignore this advice, over the course of the mesocycle you will accumulate too much fatigue in your neuromuscular system. This could be to such a degree that your CNS system will be completely flat by the day of the championship and when it counts the most!

7

Which 1RM Method Program Should You Select and Why?

The 1RM Method: 4-Week or 6-Week Program

There are two different options for running the 1RM method, the 4-Week and 6-Week options, but how do you choose which one is right for you?

It is really quite simple. If you are currently executing another strength training method that has you predominately performing intensities below 85%, then you should choose the 6-Week 1RM Method. The reason is that the muscle fibre type recruitment and specific energy systems that you are currently using are less specific to achieving a 1RM and therefore, take more time to transfer.

A very basic example might be a situation where you are currently performing a basic 5x5 protocol on a lift and then try to go straight into performing a max double. It will feel like you are going to get crushed! Basically, the lower the intensity you have been training with, the longer it takes for the neuromuscular system to be fully prepared to handle a 1RM load. In most cases, these other strength methodologies rightfully have a higher level of volume and you will benefit from a slight volume reduction throughout this phase to better allow you to effectively peak and display your true 1RM potential.

On the other hand, if you are currently executing any method that has you lifting above 85% of your 1RM regularly, then you should likely choose the 4-Week 1RM Method. The reason for this is that the muscle fibre type recruitment and energy system currently in use are more specific to a 1RM and therefore, require less time to transfer. In most cases, these other methodologies have slightly lower volumes and might only benefit from a very small reduction in volume so that you do not peak prematurely.

Regardless of the system that you are currently using, the 1RM Method helps transfer strength for achieving your true 1RM at that specific moment in time when it truly counts the most!

High Intensity High Frequency (HIHF) protocols like Smolov, Bulgarian, and other similar methods

These are great systems and I use my own hybrid variations that provide tremendous results with none of the down side. You should always be aware of a key element when executing these types of methods that can often let you down in the long run. To achieve the best possible results from training at such high frequencies using these methods, powerlifters rely on most of the training being between 67–84% of your 1RM to accommodate the high frequency of training. So, it is easy to see that these methods are in fact, not that high intensity at all.

The lower intensity that is needed to accommodate reduced recovery due to high frequency is where these methods can often let you down. You will have to train at a lower intensity for prolonged periods with these systems, and consequently, they can be said to be less specific for achieving a 1RM. If you are performing a HIFI system, you will need to better to prepare the neuromuscular system to deal with higher intensities. Simply put, it will take longer to fully transfer strength gains made in these methods to a 1RM. Hence the reason why you should use the 6 weeks method for full realisation effect to take place and this way you will be able to fully display your true 1RM potential.

Now this is where someone usually tells me I am crazy!

There is always someone who is quick to tell me that Olympic weightlifters typically train at 92–98% of their 1RM with sometimes under 48-hours of recovery time during the build-up phase before a championship competition. While this may be true, it is important to note…

…Weightlifting and Powerlifting are two very different sports!

They not only consist of vastly different movements, but the weight loads that are lifted also greatly vary. Nobody in the world can lift 350kg over their heads, but weightlifters also use different strength capabilities. Weightlifting is an expression of your dynamic 1RM (power) lifts like a "clean and jerk" motion that would normally be only about 80% of your 1RM on a squat. That is for the most elite, top-performing weightlifters. The typical weightlifter would be in the ball park of around 70% of what they can squat. Meanwhile, the complexity of the movement will always limit the load lifted. These lighter loads will still be taxing on the CNS system but in a very different way, allowing faster recovery between sessions.

Powerlifting is an expression of your *maximal strength*. For this reason, powerlifting will always have a bigger impact on the nervous system. Anyone that has ever performed any dynamic effort work for multiple sets will normally tell you they are good to go the very next day.

Probably the biggest and most important difference between weightlifting and powerlifting is the eccentric component performed on the squat and bench. In weightlifting there is very little eccentric work performed, whereas in powerlifting it is all about holding a tight, positive, controlled tempo if you are going to be successful in your attempts.

Remember the eccentric aspect is the most taxing on your recovery and this why should not just simply apply weightlifting methods to powerlifting and expect to get good results.

Anyone who states that they have successfully achieved peak condition through the implementation of a HIHF program has likely never really tapped into their true 1RM potential.

I will admit that when I first started to design the 1RM Method many years ago, I was not 100% sold on HIHF training systems or Smolov and Bulgarian style methods. At the time, I was following a more modified Westside Template/concurrent methods with intermediate and advance lifters. When working with novice lifters and other athletes from different sports, I would generally use a more block periodisation approach such as:

- Anatomical Adaptation (GPP)
- Hypertrophy (SPP)
- Strength (SPP)
- Competition Phase

Now do not get me wrong, I also used many other different training methodologies with varying results, but a modification of the Westside Template was the one for me and I am still a big fan. However, I will not go into any significant detail about the concurrent style methods, simply because this is only one of the systems I use.

The main benefit that I started to notice with lifters using HIHF methods is the increased maximal strength levels that occur in shorter periods of time. As a result, I began paying closer attention to these methodologies. Only then did I realise that even natural lifters holding down full-time jobs could benefit from these methods with certain modifications.

Please take note. I wrote *"lifters"* and not *"athletes"*. It is *powerlifters and obviously weightlifters* who can benefit from these methodologies. I am not trying to say that powerlifters and weightlifters are not athletes, but after working for over twenty years as an S&C Coach with athletes from numerous different sports, it does not take a genius-level IQ to determine the significant differences.

No athlete can perform heavy squats properly more than twice per week while still maintaining the capabilities to recover fully or to perform well enough in a related sporting skill or competition. So, the notion of performing squats 3–4 times a week for them is simply ridiculous. Of course, if you have an extended amount of time during the off session then HIHF training might be a method worth a second look.

For those of you who are looking forward to a rather lengthy layoff, you will likely end up practising your related sport at a lower level due to all the residual fatigue. Be careful, performing at a lower level due to fatigue while still maintaining very high training volume can leave you at a higher risk of sustaining injuries.

The approach for the 1RM Method is very similar regardless of the protocol you are currently using. If you are using a HFHI style system, then you will need slightly more time for a transmutation and realization effect to take place. Generally, it will takes about six weeks to transfer from most sensible HIFI methods or any method using below 85% of your estimated 1RM. If you are using a Westside Template or any concurrent style method which regularly utilises 4RM or above 85% of your 1RM, then you will only need about four weeks to fully transfer your strength gains into achieving your ultimate 1RM in competitions.

7.1 How to use the 1RM Method to peak using any method that has you performing loads below 85% (this will usually include most HIHF methods)

In many ways, transitioning to the 1RM Method can boost results substantially when the current method that you are using requires loads that are 85% or below. This is because your body will not be accustomed to the increased maximal loads after the training performed with lower intensity loads and increased volume with traditional HIHF methods.

This is why you often see many powerlifters underperforming at championships if they have been using HIHF methods based on their 8RM, 6RM or 5RM. Your body simply does not adapt well enough with only two or three exposures to the very different training loads that are required to achieve a 1RM. As a result, lifters usually need more time and exposures to the 1RM Method so that they can peak effectively and reap the benefits of increased strength gains made from these methods.

Needless to say, with the ever-growing popularity of HIHF methodologies and the great results that can be achievable over the long-term, I soon began to realise that I needed to adapt my 1RM Method to accommodate those lifters who are transitioning to my new program through other HIHF style systems.

Believe it or not, HIHF lifters need a very structured system in place to peak for a 1RM successfully. Unfortunately, most HIHF methodologies require the powerlifter to lift loads that are lower percentages of their 1RM. While this strategy generally results in better performance for your 8RM, 6RM, and even possibly your 4RM, it does nothing to improve your 1RM whatsoever. As a result, lifters using HIHF methodologies tend to underperform significantly in their 1RM, compared to what they are lifting for reps in their preparatory cycles.

Another big problem with HIHF systems concerns how to taper effectively if the lifter is accustomed to lifting 3–4 times a week on key movement patterns.

Well, keep reading! Because I am going show you how!
I would also recommend to anyone transitioning from HIHF to the 1RM Method to always perform a sprinkling of supra-maximal work in a similar motor pattern like the movements that you will be using to display your 1RM on the day of competition. Supra-maximal work might include:

- Partial Squats
- Walkouts
- Rack Holds
- Board Press

- Rack Pulls
- High box squats

Performing some supra-maximal work will help to better accustom the nervous system for the all-important 1RM. Remember to always respect the fact that your nervous system will take a bit longer to recover fully from these supra-maximal loads. *So do not overdo it!* Lift just enough to allow your body to get used to the supra-maximal weights and this way, your nervous system will be prepared to handle the increased 1RM loads. Performing as little as one or two sets post-main-exercise will do the job nicely.

This information is important because your nervous system is very sensitive. While using an HIHF method, the exposure to near maximal loads is low because of high frequencies. Therefore, these large loads essentially shock your nervous system, resulting in a limited capacity for the body to recover fully in the same timeframe between sessions. Also, it is never a bad idea to train your nervous system to handle these higher loads, as this increases your chances of hitting a new personal best during competitions. If you think about it, a new 1RM is a weight that you have never lifted in the past. Why not improve your chances by training your nervous system to handle these heavier weights now, rather than just leaving it till the day of the competition?

Just look at the successes of equipped powerlifters competing in Raw or Classic competitions. These guys win so much because their nervous systems have grown accustomed to lifting supra-maximal weights that suits and shirt allow them to handle.

When it comes to hitting a New Personal Best, the more successful competitors:

- **Still look very confident when setting up with the weight.**
- **Tend to hold the line better, increasing their chances of success even further.**
- **Have a psychological advantage over the competition of already knowing what a supra-maximal weight feels like.**

Now do not get me wrong! I am not saying to rush out and spend a small fortune buying a bunch of suits that probably will not fit, only to turn around and spend more money on another suit that probably will not work! Nor am I going to tell you to endure the same tedious process for buying a bunch of bench shirts.

If by some miracle, all of that does not annoy the heck out of you, then think about all that extra time needed on your training days for suiting up (and suiting down for that matter). How about all that extra warm-up time? What if your training partner does not show up for a bench session? Are you going to suit up all by yourself and risk the bench? Good luck with that! While you are at it, you might want to start looking for a part-time job too, because it is unlikely you will have enough time in the day to hold down a full-time career!

Okay, maybe I am being a bit *over the top!* But you can see my point right? Equipped lifting just is not practical, not for me or most of my lifters anyway, but lots of respect to those that do find the time!

Needless to say, I have learned a great deal from equipped lifting, including the many possible benefits that can apply to raw lifters. All that you have to do is take a look at your lifting program to determine where you can employ similar benefits by using bands, chains, partials, walkouts, so on and so forth, as most of the innovations came from equipped lifting to better accommodate the human strength curve.

Okay! So, what is the best training methodology?
Should you use HIFI protocols, a Westside Template, or some other form of linear block periodisation? Well, that all depends on what you "put in." If you are a complete novice with very little experience lifting weights, then a simple linear block periodisation might be the most appropriate, allowing you to focus on building a great foundation while witnessing incremental improvements week by week. On the other hand, if you are a more advanced lifter, capable of lifting insanely large loads, then your nervous system likely needs over 72-hours to recover fully between sessions. In this case, a Westside style template might be a better option.

So, what *is* the best training methodology? It is very simple. *THERE IS NO BEST METHODOLOGY!!*

As a general rule, lifters following HIHF make bigger gains over the long-term than those using other protocols. However, HIHF lifters also seem to be more prone to injury, but that is another issue entirely. The main reason that HIHF lifters tend to witness big boosts in their maximal strength levels over long term is because of the sheer amount of volume and the cumulative refinement of intermuscular coordination that comes from an increased exposure to the related movement patterns.

When these HIHF powerlifters transition to the 1RM Method, they should usually begin with slightly higher volumes because of the increased circulating anabolic hormones that their androgen receptors are used to. Higher circulating anabolic hormones are a consequence of performing higher training frequencies and overall greater volume. This is why you will need to increase the volume slightly on the 1RM Method to prevent the all-important receptors from being starved and your strength falling in this all important peaking phase.

You will also need a slightly longer tapering and peaking phase to allow your nervous system to become accustomed to handling greater loads. Meanwhile, your androgen receptors will also need to grow accustomed to the new levels of anabolic hormones produced by the 1RM Method.

MON	TUE	WED	THU	FRI	SAT	SUN
1x4 Max Four squat & Deadlift. Assistant & accessory work	Dynamic Bench. Assistant & accessory work	3	Dynamic Squat. Assistant & accessory work	1x4 Max Four bench. Assistant & accessory work	6	7
4x3 Volume triple squat. 4x3 deadlift 80% Assistant & accessory	Dynamic Bench. Assistant & accessory work	10	Dynamic Squat. Assistant & accessory work	5x3 Volume triple bench. Assistant & accessory work	13	14
1x3 Max triple squat & Deadlift. Assistant & accessory work	Dynamic Bench. Assistant & accessory work	17	Dynamic Squat. Assistant & accessory work	1x3 Max triple bench. Assistant & accessory work	20	21
5x2 Volume double squat. 5x3 Deadlift triples 90%. Assistant &	Dynamic Bench. Assistant & accessory	24	Dynamic Squat. Assistant & accessory	5x2 Volume double bench. Assistant & accessory	27	28
1x2 Max double squat & Deadlift. Assistant & accessory work	Dynamic Bench. Assistant & accessory work	2	Dynamic Squat. Assistant & accessory work	1x2 Max double bench. Assistant & accessory work	5	6
5x1 Volume single squat. 5x2 Deadlift doubles 85%. Assistant & accessory	5x1 Volume single bench Assistant & accessory work	9	10	11	12	13 Meet

6 Week 1RM Method Example

7.2 How to use the 1RM Method to peak using any method that has you performing loads above 85%

Powerlifters who use Westside and other methods with intensities above 85% tend to witness much larger improvements in the short-term on their 1RMs. This is likely due to them being more accustomed to handling weights with near maximal loads. Any system using intensities of this level will have to allow for more time between sessions for the nervous system to recover fully.

In my experience, these types of methods tend to be less beneficial in long-term strength gains, largely because the lifters following these methods have lower weekly training frequencies and lower total tonnages lifted due to the lower overall volume of work done. As we all know, the frequency of the overall volume is the key to long-term strength development.

Lifters performing these methods generally execute better 1RMs compared to their estimated 1RM%, especially compared to lifters utilizing HIFI protocols. The lower volume and less frequent training systems allows lifters to train at higher intensities and their bodies become accustomed to handling higher intensity loads like those performed in competitions. Therefore, higher intensity methods have a shorter transfer period to the 1RM Method, allowing the lifter to produce the best possible 1RM when it truly counts the most. For the most part, these methods do not produce the same long-term gains as HFHI methods for the reasons outlined above.

By utilizing methods consisting of higher intensities and lower volumes, you get more accurate feedback and a better understanding of how your body will respond to a 1RM. As a result, attempt selection is far easier and definitely more accurate. If you want to *WIN*, attempt selection is everything!

8

General Information

Because strength gains are neural in nature, the 1RM Method consists of only one mesocycle that is between 4 or 6 weeks in length stimulating full neural adaptation from previous phases. The 1RM method focuses on multiple different categories of strength training including power, functional hypertrophy, and obviously maximal strength, and therefore can be said to be a form of concurrent training.

When the level of intensity steps up, such as during the single set max effort predictor lift weeks, the volume is at its lowest to allow for the successful achievement of maximised accommodation. When performing multiple sets during the volume weeks, the reps are reduced by 1, in order to achieve ideal volume for strength gains. The increased volume generates a small overreaching effect. The volume weeks also act as a fixer to better stabilise higher intensity loads being lifted from the single set max effort predictor lift weeks.

When performing the 1RM Method, there is a linear step loading progression in intensity occurring simultaneously with an undulating decrease in volume, all of which allows your body to taper and accommodate to increased intensity stimuli needed to achieve the perfectly timed peaking effect when it counts the most.

It is my experience that most competitive organisations and coaches tend to use the max triple attempt and max double attempt as a basis of comparison for optimal attempt selections in future competitions. This is the norm, regardless of the organisation, coach or country of origin, as long as the organisation already has a real system in place that achieves consistent and substantial results at the highest levels of elite powerlifting.

I have coached countless powerlifters in championships of all kinds over the years and the lifters who use max triples and max doubles as part of their build-up always hit more of their attempts in competitions than lifters using max singles based on RPE's. The reason for this is simple. Performing max triples and max doubles coming into a competition gives lifters the best possible feedback for determining the true 1RM of which they will be capable on the day.

There are a few problems associated with only performing max singles based on RPEs in the last few weeks leading up to a competitive event.

1. Firstly, it is almost impossible to perform enough volume of work to maintain strength levels for more than a few weeks, especially for non-enhanced lifters.
2. The second and probably most important issue, is that this style of preparation for a championship is just way too subjective to get any substantive or accurate feedback regarding the correct 1RM selections on the day.

For example, let's say that you are feeling really pumped and ready to lift some singles at whatever RPE. After or even during the lift, you assume that you are performing only about 92% your true 1RM because you simply felt terrific on that particular day. In reality however, you were actually training at 95% or even 96% of your

1RM. As a result, you unintentionally created a great deal more stress on your body's nervous system that will take a considerable amount of time to bounce back from.

Subsequently, in your final week of lifting before the competition, you will be likely to select a load that is going to be substantially higher than the previous week, which you mistakenly assume will be approximately 95% to 96% of your 1RM. Once again, this will be wrong and the actual weight will be more like 98–99% of your true 1RM. Nothing good will come of training at such high intensities during the four to seven days that's generally recommended to rest for before a competition. More than likely, you will actually reduce your body's ability to perform your true 1RM when it counts the most, on the day of the powerlifting event.

The 1RM Method requires lifters to perform max triple and max double predictor lifts every other week. This gives you the opportunity to get highly accurate feedback regarding the real 1RM percentages of these lifts, identifying what your real capabilities are for determining a true 1RM for the date of the competition.

For best results, try factoring in the super-compensation effect of reduced volume after the taper and also factoring in your muscle fibre type to some degree. If you know that you are more slow twitch dominant, then you will likely be better suited to perform more reps so that your max triple might end up being at a slightly higher percentage than you anticipated.

As an example, most lifters should be targeting a good quality max triple of roughly 93% of their true 1RM. However, if you tend to be more slow twitch, then your max triple might be closer to 96% or possibly even more. Meanwhile, if you happen to be blessed with a large degree of fast twitch fibres, then your max triple might only be 91% or less of your 1RM.

Another issue of consideration, and this is seldom ever written about, is that your muscle fibre type will differ between muscle groups. Your gender and individual genetics will also have an impact on muscle fibre type distribution. I have found however, that by using the 1RM Method, over time you will develop better attempt selections, build better totals, and win more championships, regardless of your muscle fibre type.

Training with true max effort weights, not weights based on some arbitrary percentage in the weeks leading up to a competition event is very important for a number of reasons.

- By performing max effort loads, your sympathetic nervous system floods the body with a cascade of powerful hormones like adrenaline, dopamine, and cortisol, which increases membrane excitability.
- This flood of hormones helps prepare the body for the immediate loads that it is about to lift by optimising force production and ensuring that the muscle cells have enough needed energy to get the job done.
- As a result, lifting 77–87% of your estimated 1RM in the weeks or days before the competition will simply not have the same level of critically important mental and physical effects, compared to knowing that you need to hit a good max triple or a great max double. You need to experience that rush of adrenaline and know how to handle it positively. This extra psychological stress of knowing in advance that you cannot afford to miss that max triple or max double is as close as you can possibly get to the stress that you feel during a real competition.

It is important to experience this similar psychological mind set and to learn how to handle more positively the burst of adrenaline that leads to higher levels of excitement, aggression, and perhaps even a little fear. These types of emotions are completely normal and specific; they will benefit your lift once you become accustomed to them during the final phase.

LET's be honest! Achieving your ultimate 1RM is the true goal!

It is not just about peaking at the right time, performing great extrinsic mechanics, or tapping into those all-important high threshold motor units. Achieving your optimum 1RM is just as much about believing that you can and having the right frame of mind necessary to achieve it. The mind is a very powerful tool. Only by performing max triples and max doubles will you gain the confidence needed to truly believe that a new 1RM is entirely within your reach.

Trying to peak by performing a few doubles or singles at around 77–87% while also expecting to have an overall positive effect on a 1RM does not make a great deal of sense. It is like spending time studying Italian before taking the final exam for a class in Spanish. When training at 77–87% of your 1RM you are activating slightly different muscle fibre types, so the intramuscular coordination will be different. On top of that, the psychological preparation and arousal levels involved will be completely different. Now, I am not saying that you should all go out and perform a 1RM coming into competition, but what I am saying is that it is a very difficult balancing act to keep your training as sport-specific as possible, without frying the nervous system in the build-up to a 1RM.

Peaking for a 1RM is about getting close to your 1RM to stimulate a realisation effect that, ultimately, better enables maximal strength to be achieved. This method is a balancing act to which your body can adapt.

The body must be able to adapt positively to the entire amount of stress that it faces on a daily basis, not just during the workout but over the whole mesocycle. In the case of lifting weights, the body attempts to handle these stresses better by signalling the body to turn up protein synthesis after the workout. Over the long-term, this leads to increased muscle size and strength.

As you continue to lift over the course of your career, your body becomes better and better suited for handling higher and higher loads. Your bigger, stronger muscles make the weight seem easier to lift and the stress on the body decreases comparatively. Even more interestingly, research has shown that the next time you go to lift near maximal weights, your body learns and anticipates by increasing the sympathetic drive as we have mentioned before.

This all goes back to what we talked about earlier, that the brain triggers the automatic stress responses not just during periods of stress but also in anticipation of other stresses that are very sport-specific. Learning how to better manage these auto-responses in the gym, you will gain significant advantages for the competition as a result.

Important Note - transferring strength to a 1RM

Remember, you absolutely cannot expect to get any real transfer of strength without first laying down the proper foundation. If you are accustomed to performing sets of 7–8 reps over 40 sec TUT on key movements, do not expect an immediate strength transfers. It is important to understand that you have been using entirely the different energy system / muscle fibre type that will be used when performing a 1RM. Secondly, you are also recruiting the wrong motor units. After all, these are not the same motor units that you should have been tapping into for at least a few months before attempting a true 1RM optimal lift.

This is not to say that performing sets of 8–10 reps cannot produce beneficial results on accessory or even some assistance exercises. It just will not provide any immediate improvement to your 1RM, especially in such a short timeframe of 8-weeks or less (well, it might work for a novice or beginner powerlifter, but it is still not the smarter approach). Performing exercises of 20 seconds or less TUT time under tension will always produce the best improvements to your 1RM.

8.1 1RM Method: Non-Equipped Lifting & Equipped

The 1RM Method is designed with the classic / raw lifter in mind, which is the type of lifter that I predominately coach. However, I have also found that the 1RM Method to also be very effective for equipped lifters. I firmly believe, however, that the future of the sport of powerlifting is in unequipped, classic lifting and this is why I have predominantly used it with unequipped lifters.

Equipped lifting is excellent for lots of reasons, but the fact that, until only recently, there was only equipped powerlifting competitions at the international, truly elite-level, has held the sport of powerlifting back for many years. Since the IPF introduced classic / raw lifting at an international level, the sport has quite literally blown up. In my over twenty years of S&C coaching, I have never seen a sport grow so quickly.

I know powerlifting was big in the 70- 80's, but it was nothing compared to what we are accomplishing in the sport by today's standards. A large portion of the advancements and surge in popularity is largely due to women entering the sport. This may be because younger women have a healthier perception of body image compared to past generations. In fact, many of my female lifters have supported this claim.

This phenomenon may be due, in part, to female celebrities posting videos of themselves all over social media and performing squats and deadlifts to create a strong feminine physique. For the past twenty years, I have seen people from all walks of life in the powerlifting community. Rich, poor, young, old, ex-military, ex-cons, doctors, lawyers, teachers and bankers, it just does not seem to matter. Powerlifting is a sport that brings people together in a very positive way, allowing us each to reap tremendous physical, mental, and spiritual benefits.

To be honest, I found the sport somewhat lacking before the fairer sex decided to join the powerlifting party, but not anymore! In nearly every part of the country, there are nearly as many female lifters as there are male lifters and I am told that this is happening in lots of other countries around the world too. It cannot be denied that women are helping the sport of powerlifting to grow by leaps and bounds.

Other factors have had a tremendous influence also. Thanks to social media, Cross Fit and the introduction of the IPF Classics European and World Championships, more and more people are purchasing gym memberships and practising their squatting, benching, and deadlifting. It is hard to say just how big the sport is going to get!

Unfortunately, for far too many years, there has really only been competitions for equipped lifters at the international elite-level. Let's be honest, it is very hard for the average person viewing from the audience to understand why powerlifters, these incredible lifters, walk onto the competition platform like they can't move their legs properly, or when it comes to performing the bench press, why the lifters look like they are some sort of straight-jacket-clad-magician struggling his or her way to freedom.

Images like these leave a strange perception of the sport in the mind of the Average Joe. They begin to wonder, "how much did the equipment actually help that lifter and could they lift the same weight without it?"
With classic/raw lifting however, Joe Public can obviously see the massive weights that these incredible athletes are lifting while not dismissing it as, "It is just the equipment" to appease their fragile egos. In any form of athletic competition, it seems that the most popular sports are always the ones to which the Average Joe can most easily relate …and ones that do not require a lot of expensive and hard-to-find equipment!

Let's take a look at one of the most popular sporting events in the Olympics, the 100-meter sprint. Why is this sport the most globally popular when there are other sports like gymnastics or figure skating that are much more visually entertaining? In my opinion, it is because gymnastics and figure skating are incredibly difficult for most people to imagine themselves performing. These impressive athletes can almost defy gravity by flying through the air, seemingly without any effort at all. Of course, we all know that this is not the case, but most of us can never imagine ourselves performing these kinds of movements.

But we can all imagine ourselves running 100-meters at the speed of light! In fact, many of us came very close to this (or so we *imagine*) back when we were mere youngsters playing racing games with our friends in the school playground. So we can easily respect and relate to just how fast these Olympic athletes are running. I truly believe that classic/raw powerlifting will eventually gain a similar mass market appeal, which will help to improve the growth and visibility of unequipped and equipped lifting.

Please do not get me wrong. I am not ignorant to the fact that some of the best lifters in the world are equipped lifters. I just believe that the notion of international competitive unequipped lifting has mass market appeal and will only benefit the sport of powerlifting tremendously.

Mass market appeal

For more than a decade, I never found any good systems for achieving a maximal strength, competition-level 1RM. For primarily this reason, I started to experiment with my own systems before finalising my current method, the 1RM Method, which continues to be the most effective. Like I said before, the reason there are not already any good systems in place to achieve a competition-level 1RM is likely due to one thing – *MONEY!* There are loads of great programs for building maximal strength for individual reps because these programs have terrific mass market appeal and publishers and authors always want to sell a lot of books!

On the flip side, peaking for an optimum maximal 1RM effort does not offer a great deal of mass market appeal because the only athletes doing this are powerlifters or weightlifters; a very small percentage of the athletic community. Ironically, weightlifters are really performing very powerful movements that express their dynamic 1RM and powerlifters are lifting weights at maximal loads, which will not be expressed as a powerful movement because of the maximal load and time taken to lift it. Lifting weights maximally does not appeal to the masses at present, so there simply is very little effort being made to provide proven methods for peaking with the primary goal of achieving the best 1RM maximal load.

The 1RM Method is predominantly designed for unequipped lifters. If you follow all of the included information outlined for peaking and tapering, then you will never overly tax your neuromuscular system, which then allows for ideal peaking when it counts the most.

My advice for equipped lifters using the 1RM Method is to decrease the overall volume of assistance and accessory work while simultaneously factoring in a slightly longer tapering phase for your nervous system to recover fully before championships. After all, we all know that kit equipment allows for the lifting of supramaximal weights, which only generates greater stress on the nervous system which is why you will benefit from an extra day or two of full recovery before the championships.

Remember, equipped lifting utilises supramaximal weights. What I mean by this is that the weight is typically more than the average lifter can handle without the assistance of an equipped kit. Therefore, your central nervous system becomes significantly more fatigued than with standard submaximal training performed by non-equipped lifters.

Be the best you can be

I have seen and trained many athletes who have won championships. However, many have been truly disappointed because, despite walking away with the medal, they still underperformed by a mile! In fact, I have personally experienced this same level of disappointment until I really started to fine-tune my own system to achieve an optimal 1RM at the specific moment that I needed it the most. On the other hand, I have also coached lifters who have finished last in their weight class and we were still absolutely over the moon with excitement because they far exceeded their expectations by following a great plan and peaking effectively.

That's why powerlifting is such a great sport and deserves far more attention than it currently gets. Powerlifting is about far more than just building phenomenal physical strength. You will and need to become mentally stronger and emotionally confident to handle bigger weights. As a result, you become a stronger person in general and become more motivated and happier with who you are. If you want to be the best "you" that you can be, then learning and understanding your limitations while striving to overcome them is key. Powerlifting is a journey of self-discovery and self-improvement on all levels. As a coach I have found that the lifters who have the best gains are always the lifters who are humble and willing to acknowledge both their strengths *and* their weakness, whilst being mentally positive enough to continue improving, little by little.

Powerlifting is a great sport. Let's be real and stop introducing more and more different categories into the competitions (double-ply, raw with knee wraps) only so that we each win a medal and be considered a World Champion in something. There are only two categories that really count – unequipped and equipped. Stop pretending that you are a World Champion. It simply does not count if your title is in some obscure category or some dodgy federation that only a handful of people enter.

Why go through years of lifting, training, and specialised diets simply to win some stupid medal that no one gives a damn about? Deep down, you will not give a damn either because you already know that there are only one or two lifters in your class. Do you call that winning?

Continue on this path and you will only end up walking away feeling empty. You will never really feel like you have achieved anything. Let me tell you, you are missing out my friend! Everyone at the EPF or the IPF World Championships is already a champion of the country that they are representing. These lifters have earned the right to call themselves true champions, whether they rank as #1 or #16 in their respective classes. Anyone who knows anything about powerlifting will always agree that these athletes are the *Best of the Best*.

When you surround yourself with other like-minded lifters who give it their all regardless of the outcome and you perform to the best of your abilities each and every day, then, and only then, can you call yourself a true powerlifter, regardless of coming in first, second, or last.

We can't all be British, European, or IPF World Champions and that's perfectly fine! In fact, we could work out for five or six years before ever winning even a single divisional title and that's fine too! Hell, you may never win any championship whatsoever! But who cares? It is all about that incredible level of satisfaction that comes from achieving your new Personal Best during a competition.

8.2 The 1RM Method: Key Points to Consider

The key points to the system is training to succeed

If you truly want to succeed at optimising your 1RM then you need to make sure that you achieve all of your max effort predictor lifts. Do not get sucked into that old bodybuilding approach of "training to failure". Bodybuilding gets so much media attention that so many people mistakenly assume that this is the only way to train. When in reality, strength athletes rarely train to failure. We train to succeed!

The closest that you should ever get to "training to failure" is during that very last rep or perhaps the very last set. We call this "technical failure". Never complete failure.

- Failing or missing lifts will not make you stronger. Succeeding at pre-planned weights and lifts is the best way to increase strength and boost your 1RM. It also instils a very much-needed sense of self-confidence to succeed when it ultimately counts the most, at the competition!
- To get the most out of the 4-Week peaking phase you should be coming off the back of performing no more than five reps in your previous phase of training at 85% or more of your estimated 1RM. Ideally, your program will consist of lots of max triples and max doubles.
- Do not expect to come off the back of a system that has you performing eight reps and achieve a great max triple, because I guarantee that you will only shock your nervous system and potentially flatten it out for a week or more, which essentially sets you up for failure once again. Your nervous system will not be ready to handle the true max effort loads. If you are currently performing more than five reps at less the 85% of your 1RM, then you will need to follow the 6-week peaking phase instead.
- If you are performing under 75% of your estimated 1RM, then truthfully, you should spend at least four weeks getting accustomed to handling loads of at least 80% before even starting even the 6-Week peaking phase.
- It is also important to remember that if you have been performing very high volume in the week before you begin the 1RM Method, you should allow for a de-load week. I like to de-load the overall volume by about 40% while generally maintaining my intensity levels.
- The de-load week should include the entirety of your training program, rather than focussing on only dropping sets on lifts that utilise key movements, like squats, benches, and deadlifts.
- Do not be overly optimistic with your planned attempts on your max effort predictor lift sessions. Remember, strength athletes train to succeed, not to fail. Before planning your max four, triple, or double predictor lifts, stop and think. Be realistic and do not bite off more than you can chew. You are training to succeed and competing to succeed. You want 9 out of 9 on your scorecard because *THAT* is what builds big totals and *THAT* is what wins' championships.

9

Getting Started

If you are comfortable with your normal warm-up and most importantly, think it is logical, then just go with whatever you normally do to warm-up for the maximal loads. That is absolutely fine. For those who need a bit of inspiration or guidance, please check out the warm-ups provided. In more than a few cases while coaching international standard lifters, I have still manipulated the volume and attempt selections of their warm-up routine to get better results.

If you happen to suffer from tightness somewhat consistently, then I always recommend a pre-workout warm-up including some dynamic stretches to enhance your ability to perform the full range of movements comfortably and with excellent form. Remember, any form development stretching should always be a separate session entirely.

The last 1–2 phases of training before beginning the 1RM Method are very important because these are the phases from which you will get the largest levels of transfer and realisation benefits.
For best results, before starting the 1RM Method, never perform more than six reps on key movements, squat/ bench/deadlift, in your previous phase. You are trying to achieve your ultimate 1RM. If you are currently performing a higher rep range protocol that consists of five reps or above, then you will need to begin with the 6-week option of the 1RM Method protocol. If you are currently performing a rep range of less than 5 reps, then you will need to begin with the 4-week option instead.

Keep in mind, you do not want to transition from a very high rep range before beginning the 1RM Method. Make sure that the training system you are currently running before beginning the 1RM Method consists of a relative high-intensity protocol and not a high-rep bodybuilding style of system. Of course, it is perfectly acceptable to continue performing higher rep ranges on assistance and accessory exercises if that is what works best for you or your program.

The reason that the 1RM Method is based on either a 4-week or 6-week program is because we are focussing on what we call a *realisation phase*. You can only *realise* the true strength created by training that occurs in the previous phases.

Do not get me wrong. You will definitely increase strength as you go through this system, but most importantly, your body will finally be able to tap into the strength you have been building over the last few weeks, months, or even years! With the 1RM Method, I will teach you how to finally tap into your true potential while achieving your optimum 1RM at the precise moment that you need it the most, during the competition.

I have used the 1RM Method with lifters, with positive results, who were coming off the back of modified Westside Templates, high-frequency high-intensity protocols, DUP, and pretty much every system in between.

If you follow my structure properly, you will get phenomenal results! The 1RM Method is simply better than any other system of peaking that you will have ever tried in the past!

I would always recommend reading both the quick start and the complete methods before starting. There will obviously be a little repetition but the information will stick better. Once you have read both the quick start and the complete method, you can then simply refer back to the quick start if there is any basic information of which you need to remind yourself at any time whilst following the method.

9.1 Effective Warm up Strategy

General warming up information

Pre-planning your warm-up is a must! A good starting point is to take larger increases in load between your initial warm up sets and then make smaller increases in load between your final warm up sets to accommodate your attempt selections. This allows you to progress appropriately from one set to the next, until you have achieved your work weight or last warm up attempt. The warm-up sets you up for success for the remainder of the workout session. When you warm up thoroughly and properly, the chances are that your session will go well and you are far less likely to suffer from injury. Here are some important rules for warming up that I typically recommend:

GOLDEN RULES FOR STRECTHING & MOBILISATION PRE-WORKOUT

- **Pre-workout mobility and warm-up routine:** A lot of people really have the wrong idea about pre-workout warm-ups. You should not be indiscriminately moving around the floor on a foam roller or using other similar tools directly before a heavy workout. This is known to create autogenic inhabitation for up to a couple of hours, effectively creating a relaxation effect in the recently foam rolled muscles. Exercises like these reduce your ability to recruit the muscle fibre to its full potential, all of which negatively impacts your training session as well as your 1RM.
- **Dynamic stretching:** I firmly believe in dynamic stretching before training sessions and it has none of the drawbacks created by foam rollers or static or passive stretching. Dynamic stretching also enhances your ability to achieve the full range of motion required for your lift while positively stimulating the nervous system. Dynamic stretching is also known to have a very positive influence on muscle fibre recruitment during training, whilst providing necessary increases in your range of motion.
- **Body weight exercises:** Always perform some form of light, all-over body weight exercise to increase blood flow and body temperature. Perform these exercises for a minimum of eight minutes or longer, depending on several factors that might include personal preferences, the gym environment, and perhaps the gym or outside temperature.
- **Previous Injuries:** Focus on isolating any previously injured areas and perform some light exercise to increase blood flow to these areas while gently increasing ROM. If you have previous injuries, perhaps from working out, from your job, or just some sort of unforeseen mishap at home, the warm-up is even more important. Never plan to hit the gym cold. The worst thing that you could do is undergo a heavy lifting session without warming-up effectively and ignoring post-workout cool-down stretches. You might as well just skip the gym altogether. At least then you will not make the condition even worse or incur further injuries.
- **Hold a tight position in all of your lifts when warming up:** One of the most important things to remember when warming up for maximal strength loads is never, never sacrifice tightness especially when trying to achieve depth on a squat. This is a common mistake and costs lifters dearly. Many lifters will get loose in the warm-up to achieve depth prematurely in the early sets. This will only serve to un-train the tight position that is so essential for lifting true maximal weights. It is always better to do more sets at a lighter load to hit optimum depth or perform similar movement patterns that will increase the ROM in a squat. As an example, perform body weight box squats with perfect technique while gradually decreasing the height of the box or bench and therefore, increasing the ROM. Another example might be to hold the

side of the squat rack while body-weight squatting and executing perfect form of the spine and pelvis until you can roughly hit optimum depth. Then, simply transfer to the bar.

- **Be tight in your deadlifts:** It is far less common to lose tightness in your bench presses, but it does happen on the deadlift, especially in the warm up of very inflexible individuals. The same rules as with the squat apply. Just gradually increase the ROM with a similar movement or while holding a tight position with a light load. As an example, in a sumo, you might perform a few sets off the pins with a lighter weight.
- **Technique, technique, technique:** Always attack the weights with great form, even during a light warm-up, but never sacrifice technique by losing your line to increase the speed of the bar. It is important to be as dynamic and as a tight as proper form will allow. Be aware that in many cases, you may not be performing these warm-up exercises very quickly due to focussing on holding a tight position, but do not worry. As long as you focus on proper form and technique, you will still recruit fast twitch muscle fibres early in the warm-up and most importantly, charge up the nervous system to get ready for the big weights to come.

I have been coaching for nearly two decades and after assessing thousands of different powerlifters who are each following very logical but similar training protocols, I have always found that those lifters who stay injury-free and have the least cumulative niggles are always the ones who also have the least social and financial pressures. This allows them to follow strict pre-workout warm-up protocols.

Unfortunately, if you do not pay attention and resolve these steadily-increasing, intrinsically-faulty mechanics, they will likely translate into injuries that can prevent you from competing.

If you are like most of us, finding that there are just simply not enough hours in the day, then I would once again recommend isolating the problematic or niggly muscle groups while performing some light exercise, followed by some gentle stretches to increase blood flow and ROM. Regrettably, it is usually the muscles that are tight due to injury that take the biggest pounding under heavy loads and are more at risk of a recurring injury.

- **Example:** Let's say that you have a minor injury in the rotator cuff musculature. Before performing the bench or perhaps even squatting, it would be a good idea to perform some light D/B external and internal rotation exercises, followed by some mild stretches to improve blood flow and ROM.

The primary objective is to not pre-fatigue these muscle groups but simply to increase blood flow instead. I find that two or three sets of 12–14 reps using a light weight followed by some light stretching will generally do the job.

- **Example:** Another common "ailment" of powerlifters are those related to hip problems, predominantly hip flexors. As a result, I nearly always recommend doing some step-overs before squatting. Another alternative is to place small 2–5kg plate on the knees and lift your knees up-and-out-to-the-sides for two to three sets of 10–12 reps.

These are great exercises because the hip flexor musculature tends to contribute considerably when performing body weight exercise to stop us from falling back. The hip flexors do very little once the weight on the bar offsets the weight of your torso. As soon as you get near maximum weight, the hip flexors tend to suddenly start working like crazy to help stabilise the spine. Essentially, the hip musculature goes from being only slightly warmed up to being overexerted and that is why so many powerlifters tend to have lots of problems in this muscle group. That being said, the slightly wider stance adopted by powerlifters is also a contributing factor.

Specific Warm-Up for Optimal Results

It is very important that lifters execute each of the warmup sets with maximal velocity and perfect technique because you are essentially targeting the same muscle fibres that you recruit during your max effort sets.

- *Non-Specific Warm-up:* Personally, I like to perform what I call a *non-specific warm-up* first. For example, perform some mobility exercises for the hip flexors to increase blood flow, targeting areas of old injuries while also increasing fluid to the related joints involved with the lifts.

Here is a good example of a non-specific warm-up for the bench. I begin by warming up the rotator cuff musculature in the shoulder by performing some light external rotation movements. Most importantly, I am not trying to pre-fatigue these muscles because that would not benefit the soon-to-follow max effort lifting. My simple goal is to increase blood flow to the small intrinsic muscles of the shoulder therefore, decreasing the likelihood of re-injuring problematic sites while increasing fluid in the joints.

- *Specific Warm-up:* I consider a *specific warm-up* to be one that involves exercises utilising the same motor pattern as the lift that I am about to perform. For example, you might want to do some squat warm-ups to the high part of a decline bench or box, then gradually increasing the range of movement by reducing the box or bench height. Important to note, you would only increase the range of movement once you are mobile and warm enough to still perform perfect technique on each rep.

Warming up this way will give you better kinaesthetic awareness and proprioceptive feedback regarding your general technique and will only serve to benefit your workout / session considerably once you place some load on the bar. It also serves to warm-up the correct movement pattern and muscle fibres that you are about to use.

Do not waste your time and energy on rowing machines and treadmills unless a medical practitioner advises you to do so.

- *Specific Lifts:* You should only really need to warm-up for each specific lift that you are about to attempt (squat, bench, or deadlift). When you are squatting and deadlifting within the same session, then simply reduce the volume needed to warm-up for the deadlift. This reduction is because the squatting warm-up already provides a certain amount of increased blood flow to the muscles and joints used for the deadlift. That being said, there is never any harm in performing a few non-specific warm-ups that are not too overly taxing on the muscle fibres and joints that you are about to hit.
- *Rest Times Between Warm-Ups:* Generally speaking, you can keep the rest times between warm-ups down to approximately 2–3 mins until you get to 65% of your 1RM. Obviously, the smaller, lighter lifters might only require two minutes, and the bigger, stronger lifters might need three minutes or possibly more.

Anything above 70% of your 1RM results in the nervous system starting to play a larger role. So if you need to take as long as 3–4mins between sets to rest then that is okay. After all, you do not want to negatively affect nervous system recovery. With strength training, the nervous system will always need more time than the muscular system to recover fully.

Once you get to about 85% of your 1RM, you should rest at least between 4–6 mins on average. For my bigger, super-heavy powerlifters, they sometimes need even longer rest intervals.

You should keep in mind that these are not overly strict rules to warming up. This is simply a guideline that works for most powerlifters but warm-ups will vary considerably from lifter to lifter. In fact, I have witnessed a considerable amount of variation even among the elite-level lifters.

- *Proper Weight Selection:* Again, after coaching numerous elite-level lifters for some of the most competitive international championships in the world, I have also witnessed massive variations in load selection as well as rest times between warm-up sets. In general, the best lifters always use similar principles when it comes to warming up. The basic example for most elite-level lifters is they take larger weight increases and perform a larger number of reps early in the warm-up and gradually decrease the weight increases between sets and reduce reps as they get closer to their opening attempts.

I could talk about weight variations forever, so perhaps a better way to explain this concept is to show you examples for three different lifters:

1. **A smaller and lighter intermediate female lifter warming up to a max triple**
2. **A novice/intermediate 105KG class male lifter warming up to a max double**

3. **And finally, an intermediate male 74KG class lifter warming up and his 1ˢᵗ 2ⁿᵈ and 3ʳᵈ attempts selections in a championship.**

9.2 Example One: Smaller, lighter intermediate female lifter warming up for a max triple

Squat

1st Set:	Bar 20kg (44 lbs)	Reps. 6	Rest 60 seconds
2nd Set:	Bar 40kg (88 lbs)	Reps 5	Rest 120 seconds
3rd Set:	Bar 55kg (120 lbs)	Reps 4	Rest 180 seconds
4th Set:	Bar 65kg (142lbs)	Reps 3	Rest 180 seconds
5th Set:	Bar 75kg (165 lbs)	Reps 3	Rest 240 seconds
6th Set (Max Triple):	Bar 80kg (175 lbs)	Reps 3	NEW PERSONAL BEST

(Exercises using large muscle groups can generally handle greater increases in load between sets of a warm-up, as you can see from the example above.)

Bench

1st Set:	Bar 20kg (44 lbs)	Reps. 6	Rest 45 seconds
2nd Set:	Bar 30kg (65 lbs)	Reps 5.	Rest 90 seconds
3rd Set:	Bar 35kg (77 lbs)	Reps 4.	Rest 150 seconds
4th Set:	Bar 40kg (85 lbs)	Reps 3	Rest 210 seconds
5th Set (Max Triple):	Bar 42.5kg (93 lbs)	Reps 3	NEW PERSONAL BEST

(Because the bench press uses smaller muscle groups, it is generally considered wise to take slightly reduced jumps in load between sets while building up to your max effort lift.)

Deadlift

1st Set:	Bar 40kg (100lbs)	Reps. 6	Rest 60 seconds
2nd Set:	Bar 60kg (132lb)	Reps 5	Rest 120 seconds
3rd Set:	Bar 75kg (140 lbs)	Reps 4	Rest 180 seconds
4th Set:	Bar 85kg (187 lbs)	Reps 3	Rest 180 seconds
5th Set:	Bar 95kg (210 lbs)	Reps 3	Rest 240 seconds
6th Set (Max Triple):	Bar 102.5kg (225 lbs)	Reps 3	NEW PERSONAL BEST

Notice above, the number of warm sets are reduced on lifts with lower loads (bench press), whereas the lifts where greater loads are lifted (squat and deadlift) may need an increased number of warm-up sets performed. Also, please bear in mind that women generally need to do more sets nearer to their max weight in the bench press. The reason for this is because women typically have a higher proportion of slow twitch muscle fibres in the upper body than their male counterparts.

As an example, the average man executing his max double might only perform at 94–97% of his 1RM, but the average female's percentage will likely be around 96–98% or more of her 1RM.

So basically, women might need to do a few more sets nearer their maximal weight to fully warm-up the neuromuscular system to properly and safely hit a true 1RM.

Please note that this example is for a female lifter's warm-up sets for a max triple performed in training. *It is not an example of a warm-up for a competition, nor for a male lifter.* The warm-up for the female's first attempt in a meet should take a slightly different approach, depending on planned first and second attempts. Remember that *failing to plan is planning to fail*, but a plan is just a plan. You should always be prepared to change the plan to better suit your specific needs on the day of the championship.

9.3 Example Two: Novice or intermediate 105KG class male lifter warming up for a training max double

Squat

1st Set:	Bar 60kg (120 lbs)	Reps 6	Rest 90 seconds
2nd Set:	Bar 100kg (200 lbs)	Reps 5	Rest 120 seconds
3rd Set:	Bar 140kg (300 lbs)	Reps 4	Rest 180 seconds
4th Set:	Bar 170kg (350 lbs)	Reps 3	Rest 240 seconds
5th Set:	Bar 190kg (418 lbs)	Reps 2	Rest 240 seconds
6th Set:	Bar 200kg (440 lbs)	Reps 2	Rest 300 seconds
7th Set (Max Double):	Bar 210kg (462 lbs)	Reps 2	NEW PERSONAL BEST

Bench

1st Set:	Bar 50kg (110 lbs)	Reps 6	Rest 90 seconds
2nd Set:	Bar 90kg (200 lbs)	Reps 5	Rest 120seconds
3rd Set:	Bar 110kg (240 lbs)	Reps 4	Rest 180 seconds
4th Set:	Bar 125kg (275 lbs)	Reps 3	Rest 240 seconds
5th Set:	Bar 135kg (300 lbs)	Reps 2	Rest 240 seconds
6th Set (Max Double):	Bar 142.5kg (312 lbs)	Reps 2	NEW PERSONAL BEST

(Notice above, the number of warm sets are reduced on lifts with lower loads (bench press), whereas the lifts where greater loads are lifted (squat and deadlift) may need an increased number of warm-up sets performed. The bench press uses smaller muscle groups so it is generally wise to take slightly smaller jumps in load between sets while building up to your max effort lift.)

Deadlift

1st Set:	Bar 60kg (120 lbs)	Reps 6	Rest 90 seconds
2nd Set:	Bar 100kg (200 lbs)	Reps 5	Rest 180 seconds
3rd Set:	Bar 140kg (300 lbs)	Reps 4	Rest 240 seconds
4th Set:	Bar 180kg (400 lbs)	Reps 3	Rest 240 seconds
5th Set:	Bar 210kg (465 lbs)	Reps 2	Rest 300 seconds
6th Set:	Bar 230kg (510 lbs)	Reps 2	Rest 360 seconds
7th Set (Max Double):	Bar 245kg (540 lbs)	Reps 2	NEW PERSONAL BEST

As you can see from the example above, lifts that involve larger muscle groups can generally handle greater increases in load between sets for a warm-up.

Please note that this example is for a male lifter's warm-up to perform a new max double during training. *It is not an example of a warm-up for a competition, nor for a female lifter.* The warm-up for the first attempt in a meet should take a slightly different approach, depending on the planned first and second attempts.

If you are a novice powerlifter or a very nervous intermediate lifter, it is always best to have somebody check the depth of your squats while also issuing commands as a way of preparing for the competition.

To be honest, I always check the depth and general technique of even my elite-level lifters during the warm-up to give them proper and accurate feedback. This is important because, after a few days of not performing the movements and sometimes travelling to different countries, it is not uncommon to lose some kinaesthetic awareness of the movements, and as a result, mechanical mistakes can happen very easily, even with the top lifters.

It is always worth getting commands on all your final attempts, regardless of the lift. It is also a good idea to get someone to take a critical look at all your final warm up sets and give honest feedback. Better this than getting a red card.

Remember that *failing to plan is planning to fail*, but a plan is just a plan. You should always be prepared to change the plan to better suit your specific needs on the day of the competition.

9.4 Example Three:

Intermediate male 74KG lifter warming up for his competition 1st 2nd and 3rd attempts

Squat

1st Set:	Bar 60kg (120 lbs)	Reps 5	Rest 90 seconds
2nd Set:	Bar 100kg (200 lbs)	Reps 4	Rest 180 seconds
3rd Set:	Bar 130kg (285 lbs)	Reps 3	Rest 180 seconds
4th Set:	Bar 150kg (350 lbs)	Reps 2	Rest 240 seconds
5th Set:	Bar 165kg (365 lbs)	Reps 1	Rest 240 seconds
6th Set:	Bar 175kg (385 lbs)	Reps 1	Rest 300 seconds

First Attempt:	185kg (410 lbs) Roughly the same weight as his max triple.
Second Attempt:	195kg (430 lbs) Roughly the same weight as his max double.
Third Attempt:	202.5kg (445 lbs) A safe but effective third attempt.

Bench

1st Set:	Bar 40kg (90 lbs)	Reps 5	Rest 90 seconds
2nd Set:	Bar 60kg (135 lbs)	Reps 4	Rest 120 seconds
3rd Set:	Bar 80kg (175 lbs)	Reps 3	Rest 180 seconds
4th Set:	Bar 95kg (210 lbs)	Reps 2	Rest 240 seconds
5th Set:	Bar 105kg (230 lbs)	Reps 1	Rest 240 seconds

First Attempt:	115kg (255 lbs) Roughly the same weight as his max triple.
Second Attempt:	122.5kg (270 lbs) Roughly the same weight as his max double.
Third Attempt:	127.5kg (280 lbs) A safe but effective third attempt.

(Because the bench press uses smaller muscle groups, it is generally considered wise to take slightly reduced jumps in load between sets while building up to your max effort lift.)

Deadlift

1st Set:	Bar 60kg (120lbs)	Reps 5	Rest 90 seconds
2nd Set:	Bar 100kg (220 lbs)	Reps 4	Rest 180 seconds
3rd Set:	Bar 135kg (300 lbs)	Reps 3	Rest 240 seconds
4th Set:	Bar 160kg (355 lbs)	Reps 2	Rest 240 seconds
5th Set:	Bar 185kg (410 lbs)	Reps 1	Rest 300 seconds
6th Set:	Bar 200kg (440 lbs)	Reps 1	Rest 360 seconds

First Attempt:	215kg (475 lbs) Roughly the same weight as his max triple.
Second Attempt:	227.5kg (500 lbs) Roughly the same weight as his max double.
Third Attempt:	237.5kg (525 lbs) A safe but effective third attempt.

9.5 Last-Minute Tips about Warm-Ups:

- Keep your reps to six or less per set in your warm-ups for training days and 5 or less per set when you are at meets.
- The increases in weights between sets should decrease as you get closer to your estimated opener or training load.
- Remember, you are trying to minimise fatigue and maximise your ability to fire up your neuromuscular system.
- If you do need more of a warm-up, my suggestion would be to use non-specific movements that target the same musculature or joints that you are about to use for your lift. This way you will not overly stress the same motor pattern and avoid pre-fatiguing the musculature. An example of a non-specific warm-up might be the performing of a few light dumbbell flys before benching. These types of movements stretch the chest and shoulder musculature while increasing blood flow and mobilising the shoulder joints all at the same time.
- Beginners lifting less loads can rest as little as 2–3 minutes in the initial warm-up, but once you begin to approach 75% or more of your estimated 1RM, you should be resting a minimum of 3–4 minutes. As a general rule of thumb, lifters with high-strength levels, handling larger loads will need between 3–5 mins during the initial warm-up and another 5–6 mins between working sets, sometimes perhaps even more. As stated previously, this is because the nervous system takes five to six times longer than the muscles to recover fully between sets.
- When I am coaching my lifters who are competing in divisional and national championships, I often see novice and intermediate lifters treating the warm-up like a competition. A contest seems to take place to see who can make the most massive jumps between loads and still finish first. This sort of silliness is not a recipe for success. If you truly want to be *in it to win it,* then you want to plan and follow your own strict warm-up protocol.
- Do not get sucked into minimising your rest times and pre-fatiguing yourself, which will ultimately reduce your ability to lift your planned attempt. Stick to your pre-planned recipe for success in the warm-up room and show everyone your strength on the platform where it counts.
- Now after saying all of that, do not be tempted to reduce your warm-up to the point that you take out all of the mobilisation exercises regarding your most problematic joints. If you want to be the best possible lifter you can be, it is all about the long-term. That means you have to remain injury-free. A slightly longer warm-up is always better in the long run.

Employing the services of a Biomechanics coach or some type of kinesiology coach to design your warm-up can provide phenomenal results in the short and long-term. With most of the lifters with whom I have worked one-to-one over the years, I generally perform biomechanical and other FMS type screenings to better understand the lifter's limiting factors and individual faulty intrinsic mechanics.

By performing such screening, it gives me a perfect understanding of each lifter's individual needs. I can then use this information to design the most effective programs and warm-ups for each lifter. Knowing your limiting factors will identify which joints you need to mobilise or stabilise to allow for the most efficient movement possible. It also helps to identify which nerves you should mobilise to increase nerve signalling to muscle groups for enhanced recruitment and maximised strength.

10

4-WEEK 1RM METHOD

If you have been lifting less than 5 reps at more than 85% of your estimated 1RM during the previous mesocycle/phase/block, then you will need to follow the 4-Week 1RM Method approach for the full transmutation of strength that will have been developed in your previous blocks to take place.

Important information: You should always perform the 6 week 1RM Method if separating squats and deadlift into different training days regardless of training percentage. This better allows the body to better adapt to more sport specific training by squatting and deadlifting on the same day.

This is a very straightforward and easy system to follow. If you are doing the four-week prep, then this is how it works:

- The training frequency per week consists of four training sessions:
  - o 1 x lower body/max effort day, alternated between single set predictor lift weeks and decreasing volume weeks
  - o 1 x upper body/dynamic effort day, which includes hypertrophy bench
  - o 1 x lower body/dynamic effort day, which includes hypertrophy squat
  - o 1 x upper body/max effort day, alternated between single set predictor lift weeks and decreasing volume weeks

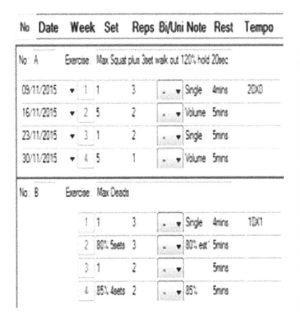

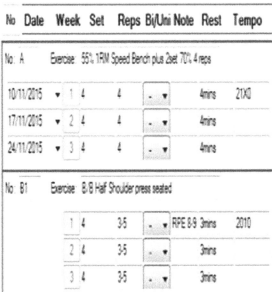

No	Date	Week	Set	Reps	Bi/Uni	Note	Rest	Tempo
No. A		Exercise	Max Bench					
13/11/2015	▾	1	1	3	▾	Single	4mins	21X0
20/11/2015	▾	2	5	2	▾	Volume	5mins	
27/11/2015	▾	3	1	2	▾	Single	5mins	
01/12/2015	▾	4	5	1	▾	Volume	5mins	
No. B1		Exercise	Decline B/B Press					
			1	3	3-5	▾	RPE 7-8	2mins	3010
			2		3-5	▾		2mins	3010
			3		3-5	▾		2mins	3010
			4		3-5	▾		2mins	3010

No	Date	Week	Set	Reps	Bi/Uni	Note	Rest	Tempo
No. A		Exercise	Max Bench					
13/11/2015	▾	1	1	3	▾	Single	4mins	21X0
20/11/2015	▾	2	5	2	▾	Volume	5mins	
27/11/2015	▾	3	1	2	▾	Single	5mins	
01/12/2015	▾	4	5	1	▾	Volume	5mins	
No. B1		Exercise	Decline B/B Press					
			1	3	3-5	▾	RPE 7-8	2mins	3010
			2		3-5	▾		2mins	3010
			3		3-5	▾		2mins	3010
			4		3-5	▾		2mins	3010

The volume in max effort days changes each week. These sessions should also include some accessory exercises and possibly a small amount of assistance work if needed.

The frequency remains the same until the last week. Then on the last week, you simply drop the dynamic effort days, further decreasing the volume. You will then only perform the two max effort sessions on the last week; one lower body and one upper body.

You will squat and deadlift on the same lower body day, which is specific to the sport, as you will need to know what level of fatigue the squat will create to maximise your 1RM capabilities on the deadlift. Normally, lifters in competitions get a few hours between the squat and the deadlift, but there is no guarantee. So be prepared and know what you can handle in case the break between your squats and deadlifts is shorter than expected.

- You will perform the bench separately, which is not specific to the sport of powerlifting. However, performing the squat first will not create any real fatigue for the bench so they do not need to be trained on the same day as the squat and deadlift. In addition, because the bench movements target smaller muscle groups than the squat and deadlift, you essentially recover much faster. Consequently, when programming for the final week leading up to the championship, bench press should be performed closer to the competition day compared to the squat and deadlift to avoid premature super-compensation.
- If you are transitioning off of the back of a high-intensity high-frequency (HIHF) system or any type of system where you are squatting or benching more than twice a week, then I recommend adding some more volume to your dynamic squat and bench sessions when performing the 4-Week Phase of the 1RM Method. 3–4 sets of 3–4 reps at 70–75% of your 1RM will do the job. This is important because your body will already be accustomed to much more volume and you do not want to taper prematurely.

When adding extra volume to a dynamic session, it is essential to train *under* 80% of your estimated 1RM to ensure not to over-emphasise the nervous system involvement and subsequently, temporarily impair the necessary recovery which would negatively affect your next max effort session.

In general, I recommend training between 70–75% of your 1RM and for no more than 3–4 reps. The reason that you should rarely exceed four reps during the peaking phase is because you might accidentally begin to "train out" the correct motor pattern that you are working so incredibly hard to maintain. By training with higher reps during a peaking phase, you start to recruit more slow-twitch muscle fibre while simultaneously corrupting your body's ability to recruit from those crucial high-threshold motor units, which are so very responsible for achieving an optimum 1RM.

Another issue with training at lower percentages with higher rep ranges to increase volume is that this often over stimulates slow twitch muscle fibres during the peaking phase for optimal 1RM. You essentially do not want any possibility of fast twitch fibres being converted to more oxidative muscle fibres. Nor do you want to confuse motor unit recruitment and in turn, possibly corrupt the correct motor pattern, which is essential for achieving your ultimate 1RM.

So, when adding extra volume, I recommend training between 70–75% at maximum speed with only 3–4 reps. This system will still recruit fast twitch muscle fibre while not overly taxing the nervous system, allowing you to be fully prepared for your all-important max effort sessions.

10.1 QUICK START

During the first week of the 4-week realisation phase, you need to perform only 1 set at 3RM. In some ways, this is one of the most important weeks of the entire 1RM Method because you really need to focus on getting it right when building up to your correct 3RM. This important step in the system defines the correct load for next week and for future weeks to follow. You do not want to build up too slowly in the warm up and risk pre-fatiguing yourself because this will lead to you being unable to perform your true 3RM. Lastly, you should not increase the load between warm up attempts to greatly, so as to not allow your neuromuscular system ideal priming between attempts. You could overshoot your 3RM.

I cannot stress this next point strongly enough. When performing the 1RM Method, *TECHNIQUE IS KING!* Proper technique is the only way that you can be sure that your max and volume efforts weeks will truly transfer over to your best possible 1RM.

Week 1 of the 4 week 1RM Method, Single Set Max Triple Predictor Lift performed on Squat Bench and Deadlift

- The first microcycle of the 4-Week realisation phase is a max triple predictor lift. The weight should be roughly the same weight that you expect to use on your first attempt on the day of competition. Again, this lift needs to be a technically-sound triple. The third rep might get a little ugly or can even be a bit of a grind, but this should definitely not occur on the first or second rep. All three reps must be technically-sound because the ultimate goal is to hit a technically-sound new Personal Best max triple.

Example of training frequency, sets, reps and percentages in week 1:

Monday: Single set max effort triple predictor lift performed on squat and deadlift only. (A) Exercise – max effort triple squat 90–94% 1RM 1 x 3 reps. (B) Exercise – max effort deadlift 90–94% 1RM 1 x 3 reps, plus assistant and accessory exercises.

Tuesday: (A) Exercise – dynamic bench 50–55% 1RM 4 x 3–4 reps. (B) Exercise – hypertrophy bench 4 x 3–4 reps 70–75%, plus assistant and accessory exercises.

Wednesday: Off.

Thursday: (A) Exercise – dynamic squat 50–55% 1RM 4 x 3–4 reps. (B) Exercise – dynamic deadlift 50–55% 1RM 4 x 3 – 4 reps, plus assistant and accessory exercises.

Friday: Single set max effort triple predictor lift performed on the bench only. (A) Exercise – max effort bench 90–94% 1RM 1 x 3reps, plus assistant and accessory exercises.

Week 2 of the 4 week 1RM Method, Volume Double performed on only the Squat and Bench

- The second week, or the second microcycle, is a volume double week. Simply drop one rep from your 3RM predictor lift and perform five sets of double reps on the squat and bench only. For example, if your 3RM is 400 lbs, then you will now perform only two reps of 400 lbs for 5 sets. Your goal is to execute between 8–10

No	Date	Week	Set	Reps	Bi/Uni	Note	Rest	Tempo
No: A	Exercise: Max Squat plus 3set walk out 120% hold 20sec							
	09/11/2015	1	1	3	-	Single	4mins	20X0
	16/11/2015	2	5	2	-	Volume	5mins	
	23/11/2015	3	1	2	-	Single	5mins	
	30/11/2015	4	5	1	-	Volume	5mins	
No: B	Exercise: Max Deads							
		1	1	3	-	Single	4mins	1X1
		2	80% 5sets	3	-	80% est	5mins	
		3	1	2	-		5mins	
		4	85% 4sets	2	-	85%	5mins	
No: C	Exercise: High Rack pull							
		1	2	3	-	RPE 8-9	5mins	2011
		2	2	3	-		5mins	
		3	2	2	-		5mins	
		4	2	2	-		5mins	

No	Date	Week	Set	Reps	Bi/Uni	Note	Rest	Tempo
No: A	Exercise: 55% 1RM Speed Bench plus 2set 70% 4 reps							
	10/11/2015	1	4	4	-		4mins	21X0
	17/11/2015	2	4	4	-		4mins	
	24/11/2015	3	4	4	-		4mins	
No: B1	Exercise: B/B Half Shoulder press seated							
		1	4	3-5	-	RPE 8-9	3mins	2010
		2	4	3-5	-		3mins	
		3	4	3-5	-		3mins	
No: B2	Exercise: Supernated pull ups + KG							
		1	4	5-7	-	RPE 8-9	3mins	2010
		2	4	5-7	-		3mins	
		3	4	5-7	-		3mins	
No: C1	Exercise: Kneeling Scap plane cable external rotator							
		1	3	8-10	-	RPE 6-7	90mins	3010
		2	3	8-10	-		90mins	
		3	3	8-10	-		90mins	
No: C2	Exercise: Bilateral D/B Rows on 30° bench							
		1	3	5-7	-	RPE 8	90sec	2010
		2	3	5-7	-		90sec	
		3	3	5-7	-		90sec	

reps with a minimum total volume of 8 reps. If you have a technically-sound max predictor lift and are still struggling to perform all five sets of doubles, then go ahead and drop a rep to perform only a single rep for the last few sets if needed. Example:

If you are struggling to achieve the recommended volume of reps prescribed, please see the example below:

Example

- Set #1: 2 reps
- Set #2: 2 reps
- Set #3: 2 reps
- Set #4: 1 rep
- Set #5: 1 rep (achieving one less rep)
- Total reps achieving over the minimum volume threshold of 8 reps in total

No: A — Exercise: Box Squat 55%

Date	Week	Set	Reps	Bi/Uni	Note	Rest	Tempo
12/11/2015	1	4	4	-		4mins	21X0
19/11/2015	2	4	4	-		4mins	
26/11/2015	3	4	4	-		4mins	

No: B — Exercise: Speed Deadlift 55% pluss chains

Date	Week	Set	Reps	Bi/Uni	Note	Rest	Tempo
		1	4	4	-	4mins	10X1
		2	4	4	-	4mins	
		3	4	4	-	4mins	

No: C — Exercise: B/B squat no box 70% 1m

Date	Week	Set	Reps	Bi/Uni	Note	Rest	Tempo
		1	3	3	-	70% 1m	3mins	3010
		2	3	3	-	70% 1m	3mins	
		3	3	3	-	70% 1m	3mins	

No: D1 — Exercise: D/B RDL

Date	Week	Set	Reps	Bi/Uni	Note	Rest	Tempo
		1	3	5-7	-	RPE 7	90sec	3010
		2	3	5-7	-		90sec	
		3	3	5-7	-		90sec	

No: D2 — Exercise: TKE

Date	Week	Set	Reps	Bi/Uni	Note	Rest	Tempo
		1	3	10-12	-	RPE 8	2mins	2011
		2			-		2mins	
		3			-		2mins	

No: A — Exercise: Max Bench

Date	Week	Set	Reps	Bi/Uni	Note	Rest	Tempo
13/11/2015	1	1	3	-	Single	4mins	21X0
20/11/2015	2	5	2	-	Volume	5mins	
27/11/2015	3	1	2	-	Single	5mins	
01/12/2015	4	5	1	-	Volume	5mins	

No: B1 — Exercise: Decline B/B Press

Date	Week	Set	Reps	Bi/Uni	Note	Rest	Tempo
		1	3	3-5	-	RPE 7-8	2mins	3010
		2		3-5	-		2mins	3010
		3		3-5	-		2mins	3010
		4		3-5	-		2mins	3010

No: B2 — Exercise: Strate Arm pos flys

Date	Week	Set	Reps	Bi/Uni	Note	Rest	Tempo
		1	3	5-7	-	RPE 7	3mins	3010
		2		5-7	-		3mins	3010
		3		5-7	-		3mins	3010
		4		5-7	-		3mins	3010

No: C1 — Exercise: B/B Tricep ext

Date	Week	Set	Reps	Bi/Uni	Note	Rest	Tempo
		1	3	5-7	-	RPE 7	90sec	2010
		2	3	5-7	-		90sec	2010
		3	3	5-7	-		90sec	2010
		4	3	5-7	-		90sec	2010

No: C2 — Exercise: Inverted pull ups supine grip

Date	Week	Set	Reps	Bi/Uni	Note	Rest	Tempo
		1	3	5-7	-	RPE 8	90sec	2011
		2	3	5-7	-		90sec	2011
		3	3	5-7	-		90sec	2011
		4	3	5-7	-		90sec	2011

Important Information: You will notice that I do not mention deadlifting on the volume double week. The reason for this is that after performing 5 sets of doubles on the squat at anywhere between 90–94% 1RM you will never be able to perform quality sets of deadlift at similar intensity.

For this reason, you simply perform 4 sets of deadlifts at 80% for triples, this allows you to maintain good form and not over stress your neuromuscular system so you are able to recover optimally for your next, all-important, max effort predictor lift on the squat and deadlift.

Example of training frequency, sets, reps and percentages in week 2:

Monday: (A) Exercise – volume doubles squat 90–94% 1RM 5 x 2 reps. (B) Exercise – deadlift will be performed at 80% 1RM 4 x 3 reps, plus assistant and accessory exercises.

Tuesday: (A) Exercise – dynamic bench 50–55% 1RM 4 x 3–4 reps. (B) Exercise – hypertrophy bench 4 x 3–4 reps 70–75%, plus assistant and accessory exercises.

Wednesday: Off.

Thursday: (A) Exercise – dynamic squat 50–55% 1RM 4 x 3–4 reps. (B) Exercise – dynamic deadlift 50–55% 1RM 4 x 3–4 reps, plus assistant and accessory exercises.

Friday: (A) Exercise – volume doubles bench 90–94% 1RM 5 x 2 reps, plus assistant and accessory exercises.

Remember, we all get sick or have a bad day from time to time. So even if you cannot achieve the minimum amount of volume of 8 reps, it is far more important to perform high-quality technically-sound reps than achieving the desired volume threshold.

One thing you should never do is add another set to the volume weeks if you have already achieved minimum volume required. This can negatively affect your nervous system's recovery for next week's max double session.

Week 3 of the 4 week 1RM Method, Single Set Max Double Predictor Lift performed on Squat, Bench and Deadlift.

• During the third microcycle, you perform your single set max double lifts. The weight should be roughly the same weight that you expect to use on your second attempt on the day of competition. Again, this lift needs to be a technically-sound double. When executing this load at a competition as your second attempt, it will build a good total and give you all of the accurate feedback needed to make the right decision for establishing your true 1RM for the day of the championship.

Example of training frequency, sets, reps and percentages in week 3:

Monday: Single set max effort double predictor lift performed only on squat and deadlift. (A) Exercise – max effort double squat 94–97% 1RM 1 x 2 reps (B) Exercise – max effort double deadlift 94–97% 1 x 2 reps, plus assistant and accessory exercises.

Tuesday: (A) Exercise – dynamic bench 50–55% 1RM 4 x 3–4 reps (B) Exercise – hypertrophy bench 4 x 3–4 reps 70–75%, plus assistant and accessory exercises.

Wednesday: Off.

Thursday: (A) Exercise – dynamic squat 50–55% 1RM 4 x 3–4 reps (B) Exercise – dynamic deadlift 50–55% 1RM 4 x 3–4 reps, plus assistant and accessory exercises.

Friday: Single set max effort double predictor lift performed only on the bench. (A) Exercise – max effort bench 94–97% 1RM 1 x 2 reps, plus assistant and accessory exercises.

WEEK 4 (FINAL WEEK) of the 4 week 1RM Method, Volume Singles performed on only the Squat and Bench

• The fourth and final microcycle is a volume single week. Perform 4–5 sets of singles using your max double load. Week 4 is an excellent time to pull together all of the technical and psychological aspects for your lifts. Even performing the lifting movements under commands can be of great benefit to all lifters from novices, all the way up to World Class Champions. Remember, technique is always paramount! If you start grinding on the third or fourth set of this final week, then it is likely time to throw in the towel and call it a day!

Important Information: You will notice that I do not mention deadlift on the volume single week. This is because after performing 5 sets of singles on the squat, at anywhere between 94–97% you will be unable to perform quality sets of deadlift at similar intensity.

For this reason, you simply perform 3–4 sets of deadlifts at 85% for doubles. This allows you to maintain good form, without over stressing your neuromuscular system and therefore, enabling you to recover optimally for the championship.

Example of training frequency, sets, reps and percentages in week 4:

Monday: (A) Exercise – volume singles squat 94–97% 1RM 5 x 1 rep (B) Exercise – deadlift performed at 85% 1RM 4 x 2 reps, plus only a small amount of accessory exercises if needed.

Tuesday: (A) Exercise – volume singles bench 94–97% 1RM 5 x 1 rep, plus only a small amount of assistant and accessory exercises if needed.

Wednesday: Off.

Thursday: Off.

Friday: Off.

Saturday: Off.

Sunday: Championships

MON	TUE	WED	THU	FRI	SAT	SUN
9 1x2 Max Triple squat, 1x2 max triple deadlift Assistant & accessory	*10* Dynamic Bench Assistant & accessory work	*11*	*12* Dynamic Squat Assistant & accessory work	*13* 1x3 Max Triple bench Assistant & accessory work	*14*	*15*
16 5x2 volume double squat, 5x3 deadlift triples 80's Assistant & accessory	*17* Dynamic Bench Assistant & accessory	*18*	*19* Dynamic Squat Assistant & accessory work	*20* 5x2 volume double bench Assistant & accessory work	*21*	*22*
23 1x2 Max Double squat, 1x2 max double deadlift & accessory	*24* Dynamic Bench Assistant & accessory work	*25*	*26* Dynamic Squat Assistant & accessory work	*27* 1x2 Max double bench Assistant & accessory work	*28*	*29*
30 5x1 Volume singles squats, 4x2 deadlift doubles at 85%	5x1 volume singles bench Assistant & accessory work					Rest or...

As you can see, this monthly plan (mesocycle) allows 6 days of full recovery between squats and deadlifts and 5 days of full recovery between benches. The mesocycle outlined above will generally better suit intermediate competitors. Novices lifting lower loads will generally benefit from less recovery days in the final microcycle, whereas advanced competitors lifting very large loads may benefit from adding more recovery days in the final microcycle.

Please refer to the training frequency section for more detailed information on how to organise the last month of training (mesocycle) for effective peaking.

Ideal minimum volume is between 4–5 reps, but as I mentioned before, it is important to remember that we all get sick or have a bad day from time to time. So even if you cannot achieve the minimum amount of volume, it is far more important to perform high-quality, technically-sound reps than to achieve your minimum volume threshold. Remember if you start grinding out reps, listen to your body, it is time to stop, call it a day and save yourself for the championships.

10.2 Complete 4 Week 1RM Method

<u>Week 1</u> of the 4 week 1RM Method, single set max triple predictor lift performed on Squat, Bench and Deadlift

If you have been performing 85% or over your estimated 1RM on the key lifts for which you wish to peak, then you should begin by performing the 4 week 1RM Method.

When executing the single set Max Effort Triple Predictor Lift, always focus on performing high-quality reps with proper technique. The only rep in this max effort single set that could or should be a bit of a grind will be the final, third rep. If you are grinding out your first or second rep, then you will never achieve the maximum positive effects for adaptation during the volume double week.

If your attempt selection is incorrect and you are grinding out badly and do not think you can successfully get your second rep, simply rack the bar, rest 6–8 mins and then drop the weight on the bar by 3–5%. If you are grinding out on your second rep and do not think you can do your third rep, then drop the weight by 2.5% or if you were roughly lifting 5% less in your last warm up set, then rack the bar and simply take this number as your max triple predictor lift. It is very important to note, you only have one second shot at getting the attempt selection right. Do not ever attempt to try more than two max effort attempts on predictor lift week as this will create too much volume from which to recover positively. Sometimes you will find that as long as you did not grind out too badly and create energy leaks, your reduced second attempt at a predictor lift will go incredibly well, and this is more than likely because of the post-activation potentiation effect from the previous set. If you honestly do not think you have another attempt in you, simply subtract 5% and call this your max effort triple predictor lift. It is important to try not to make these same mistakes again during the coming single set Max Double Predictor Lift week, as your goal is to try and get each attempt selection spot on. Getting attempt selection spot on in training will help you to become better at attempt selection on the all-important competition day. It is important to adhere to the protocols of the 1RM Method as strictly as possible, right from the very beginning.

<u>Week 2</u> of the 4 week 1RM Method, volume doubles performed on only the Squat and Bench

Take the weight you performed on your Max Triple Predictor Lift and perform 5 sets of doubles on the Squat and Bench in this volume week.

On this the second week of the 4 week 1RM Method it is important to note that you will not be performing deadlifts at the same load as you did in the previous week on the single set max effort triple predictor lift. This is because although it is important to get used to handling some fatigue from the single set predictor lifts for your training to be sport specific, it will be practically impossible and a bad idea, to lift large loads post volume double squats. Deadlifting with the same loads as week one after the 5 sets of squat doubles would not be specific to the sport of powerlifting as you will never normally be exposed to such a large level of volume and fatigue before attempting a 1RM deadlift in a championship. If you are foolish enough to try and perform heavy deadlifts, post volume squat, you are likely to train with poor technique, and may even start to train out a good motor pattern. You may even create so much cumulative fatigue that you negatively affect your CNS, making you unable to perform the all-important single set max effort double predictor lift in the following weeks training.

IMPORT INFORMATION – only perform 80% of your estimated 1RM deadlift for 4 sets of 3 reps in week 2

In week two volume double squats and bench, simply take the weight you performed on your max effort triple predictor lift on Squat and Bench, drop 1 rep and perform 5 sets of doubles with this weight in this volume week.

During the execution of the volume double week, you should never experience a bad first or second set. Things might begin to get tough around the end of the fourth set, but the fifth set is when you should start really feeling the effects. If, however, something happens and you begin experiencing bad sets earlier than expected, then this is normally a sign of perhaps an oncoming cold or flu, lack of quality sleep, lack of adequate nutrition, or very high stress levels resulting from your daily life. The only other reason this can happen is if you are performing technically poor lifts or low-quality reps on your max effort predictor lift.

This is why it is always a big mistake to be grinding out your reps when performing your predictor lift during the 1RM Method, as the weight in the following volume doubles week will be too heavy to achieve positive adaptation. Meanwhile, trying to grind out five sets of volume doubles at this load will only have extremely negative impacts on the strength adaptation and peaking that should be taking place.

So, let's say that you make one of these mistakes and your third or fourth sets are a real grind. Simply drop one rep off of each set that you have left and perform quality singles instead. If needed, simply add-on another set, thereby performing a total of six sets instead of the recommended five. By making this small modification you still achieve the minimum threshold volume of between 8–10 reps.

There may come a time when you cut reps from doubles to singles and still think you are grinding reps out badly and so are not achieving good quality. If this happens, then you should probably just cut your losses and drop the weight by 2.5% so you can perform quality technique for reps at RPE 9, striving for a minimum total volume of 8–10 reps. Then next week, focus on performing a better quality single set max double at RPE 10, while trying not to make the same mistakes.

Remember, the minimum volume threshold in this volume week is, 8–10 reps at between 90–94% of your 1RM. Good quality reps are more important than volume, so it is better to cut sets even if you probably will not achieve minimum volume threshold.

Week 3 of the 4 week 1RM Method, single set max double predictor lift performed on Squat, Bench and Deadlift.

When executing the single set Max Effort Double Predictor Lift week, always focus on performing high-quality reps with proper technique. The only rep in this max effort single set that could or should be a bit of a grind will be the final, second rep. If you are grinding out your first, then you will never achieve the maximum positive effects for adaptation during the volume single week.

If your attempt selection is incorrect and you are grinding out badly and do not think you can successfully get your second rep, rack the bar, rest 6–8mins, and then drop the weight on the bar by 3–5%. If you were roughly lifting 5% less in your last warm up set, then rack the bar and simply take this number as your max double predictor lift. It is very important to note that you only have **one** second shot at getting attempt selection right. Do not ever attempt to try more than two max effort attempts on a predictor lift week as this will create too much volume to recover from positively. Sometimes you will find that, as long as you did not grind out badly and create energy leaks, your second attempt at a predictor lift will go incredibly well, this is more than likely because of the post activation potentiation effect from the previous set. If you honestly do not think you have another attempt in you, then subtract 5% and call this your max effort double predictor lift. It is important to adhere to the protocols of the 1RM Method as strictly as possible, right from the very beginning.

Once again, I must stress that when executing the single set max double week, always perform high-quality reps. The only rep in the set that could or should be a bit of a grind is the second rep, or you will never achieve the maximum positive effects during the following volume single week. It is a big mistake to grind out your first rep when performing this stage of the 1RM Method, the max double week, as the weight in the following volume single week will be too heavy to achieve maximum positive adaptation. Meanwhile, attempting to grind out five sets of singles at this load will only have extremely negative impacts on strength adaptation and peaking that should take place in preparation for the championship.

WEEK 4 (THE FINAL WEEK) of the 4 week 1RM Method, volume singles performed on only the Squat and Bench

Take the weight you performed on your Max Double Predictor Lift and perform 5 sets of single reps under commands on the squat and bench only.

On this final week of the 1RM Method it is important to note, you will NOT be performing deadlifts at the same load as you did in the previous week on the single set max effort double predictor lift. This is because, although it is important to get used to handling some fatigue from the single set predictor lifts for your training to be sport specific, it will be practically impossible, and a bad idea, to lift large loads post volume double squats. Deadlifting with the same loads as week three after the 5 sets of squat singles would not be specific to the sport of powerlifting as you will never normally be exposed to such a large level of volume and fatigue before attempting a 1RM deadlift in a championship. If you are foolish enough to try and perform heavy deadlifts post volume squat, you are likely to train with poor technique and may even start to train out a good motor pattern. You may even create so much cumulative fatigue that you negatively affect your CNS, making you unable to perform your ultimate 1RM in competition.

<u>IMPORT INFORMATION</u> – only perform 85% of your estimated 1RM deadlift for 3- 4 sets of good quality doubles. If you start grinding out, call it a day, regardless of sets or reps completed.

During the execution of the volume single week, you should never experience a bad first or second set. Things might begin to get tough around the third or fourth set, but the fifth set is when you should really start feeling the effects. If, however, something happens and you begin to start experiencing bad sets earlier than expected, then listen to your body and call it a day. As long as you have performed three singles under commands, you will have achieved the minimum volume effective dosage. If you have not performed a minimum of three singles before you are grinding out, then you will need to look at dropping the weight by 2.5% depending on how the lift looked. It is very important to remember in this taper week that the moment you start to grind, it is time to either call it a day, or if you have not performed at least three singles, then time to drop the weight.

Trying to grind out five sets of volume singles at this load will only have extremely negative impacts on strength adaptation and peaking that should take place.

Remember the minimum volume threshold in this volume week is 3–5 reps at between 94–97% of your 1RM. Good quality reps are more important than volume, so it is better to cut sets, even if you probably will not achieve the minimum volume threshold.

BUT REMEMBER! In this FINAL WEEK, *"less is MORE!"* So if it gets really tough by the third or fourth set, call it a day and save your energy for the meet.

The Final Week: Taper Week...

In the final lower and upper body max effort volume sessions, you will be predominately focussing on your competition lifts. It is entirely acceptable to perform a certain amount of isolation accessory exercises that only target small muscle groups because these will not create a great deal of fatigue. Recovery from these types of exercises also occurs at a much faster rate than exercises targeting large muscle groups. Most importantly, you should also walk away from these workouts feeling like you could have done more.

Remember, this is not the time to grind out lifts or even, in some cases, perform assistance exercises. This is the time to allow the body to super-compensate if the ultimate goal is to hit a new Personal Best at the up and coming championship.

If you have lower strength levels, then you will not need as many days for your nervous system to recover fully and super-compensate.

Also, because lifters with lower strength levels tend to tax their nervous system to a far lesser degree, they are far more likely to suffer from a de-training effect more quickly. This is another reason to take less time off before a competition.

Most lifters entering a competition have spent several weeks or even months training extremely hard to boost maximal strength levels. One easy week is not going to erase all of your hard work and progress. Instead, these last few days will allow your body to fully realise and showcase all of that hard work. So trust the work that you have already put in and give your body a chance to reward you for your past efforts.

10.3 To sum it all up...

The 1RM Method is all about training to succeed, which is exactly what you are going to do at a competition because your goal should always be to get 9 out of 9.

If you do not have the energy or capacity to finish necessary sets, then walk away. There is no shame here. It is more important to be safe. This is especially true for accessory and assistance work. Never try and increase the volume on another day so that you can still attain your projected weekly volume or target. This is a *BIG MISTAKE* in any phase of training, but most especially during a peaking phase because the cumulative fatigue will negatively affect your performance in coming sessions. If you do not feel that you can do it, *do not!* It is always best to cut your losses and have a lower volume day by dropping sets on your assistant or accessory work. Always listen to your body.

With the 1RM Method, there is a certain amount of built-in flexibility. There is nothing wrong with completely dropping certain dynamic effort sessions if you need the rest. In fact, the only sessions that you simply cannot miss under any circumstances are the max effort sessions, but obviously, the dynamic and functional hypertrophy sessions are very important too. Your body sees them, to some degree, as active recovery days.

Let's say, for some reason, you simply cannot perform the max effort predictor lift or volume session on the day you have planned due to sickness or other issues. Normally, the best thing to do in this scenario is to first drop the dynamic effort and functional hypertrophy session that was planned. This is very important in a peaking phase as it will not be possible to recover positively with under 48-hours between max effort sessions.

By scrapping the dynamic session, it will give you more flexibility to move your session within the microcycle. The key point is to preferably make sure you have at least **72-hours** between max effort lifting and at least 48-hours between performing dynamic effort and functional hypertrophy sessions.

For instance, take the following training frequency:

*   **Monday** – max effort predictor lift or max effort volume session on squat and deadlift
*   **Thursday** – dynamic and functional hypertrophy session on squat and deadlift

If you are unable to perform the max effort predictor lift or max effort volume session on Monday, then you would drop the Thursday session and perform the max effort session on Tuesday, Wednesday or Thursday. Tuesday or Wednesday is preferable as this would give you between 5 and 6 full days recovery before your next max effort session on the following Monday, as opposed to only 4 to 5 days.

72-hours between max effort sessions should be the bare minimum and with anything less it is best to skip the session completely. If this was a max effort predictor lift, you will have to just use an estimated 3RM or 2RM based on the performance of your previous lift.

Do not forget to always pay close attention to your stress levels, both specific and non-specific. Let's say that during one of the weeks of training you have a great deal of personal and work-related stress in your life. You might need to consider dropping one dynamic/hypertrophy session just to give your nervous system time to fully recover.

10.4 Trouble shooting

If you are feeling beat up and tired, the first thing to do is to consider dropping or reducing the amount of assistance and accessory exercises in your program. This is very important if you want to be successful and achieve your ideal peak and achieve your ultimate 1RM in competition. The first exercises to drop or reduce should be your assistance exercises. This is the exercise that uses similar motor patterns to the movement you are hoping to peak.

So if you are feeling mentally, physically, and emotionally drained, drop or reduce some of these exercises first to reduce the negative impact on your nervous system and achieve a better quality recovery.

Do's and Don'ts

- On the day before the competition, try not to think about lifting or the competition whatsoever. Also try to avoid conducting any sort of visualisation techniques as this will only increase your levels of sympathetic nervousness. Believe me, nothing good will come of this. Most likely, you will just experience a very restless night's sleep due to overstimulated sympathetic and under-stimulated parasympathetic nervous systems. This imbalance will only lead to feeling fatigued on the crucial day of competition.
- I always tell my lifters to make sure to turn the lights off, or at least, dim them to a lower level for a good few hours before ultimately planning to fall asleep. Scientific research shows that low lighting better stimulates the pineal gland, which produces the chemical melatonin that positively affects the modulation of sleep patterns.
- I also recommend that lifters avoid trying to force themselves to go to sleep *too* early. This rarely works and is usually futile and a waste of mental energy. You will likely end up lying in bed for perhaps several hours trying to fall asleep. The better option is simply to turn the lights down low or completely off while keeping the room temperature cool (not cold) and getting into some very comfortable sleeping clothes.
- Perhaps the most important piece of advice that I can offer is to only go to bed when you actually feel tired. Remember, staying up a bit later while still achieving five or six hours of good quality sleep the night before a meet is still much better than getting a full eight or nine hours of broken, restless sleep.

If you try these useful *Do's and Don'ts* and sleep still eludes you, do not get too down on yourself. Certainly do not start thinking that tomorrow's competition is going to be a huge bust! Far too many times I have witnessed powerlifters arriving at a competition bleary-eyed after having suffered miserably on an excruciatingly long airline flight that was either previously delayed or cancelled, and yet they still managed to achieve a new Personal Best! So relax, as you have done all the hard work, it is now time to show everyone, and more importantly, yourself, just how strong you are.

From my over twenty years of experience with coaching and prepping powerlifters for competitions, missing a good night's sleep does not ultimately have that much effect on most lifters' performances. Sleep is kind of like training, in the sense that missing one session here or there will not automatically make you weak, but cumulatively it will have a tremendous negative impact on competitive performances.

After reviewing the HRV data analysis of lifters, I find that those who tend to naturally possess a more nervous disposition usually benefit greatly from staying busy in the final days leading up to a championship. In short, keeping busy makes them perform better on the day of the competition. This is probably because they are not sitting around worrying, essentially wasting loads of mental energy that is useful to win the medal. After all, worrying causes stress and my current HRV data analysis positively supports these findings.

Visualisation techniques can be extremely useful if they are performed at the appropriate times, but they can be very negative if you spend way too much time every day visualising your squats technique or the competition itself. Interesting to note: If your body has been exposed to consistent heavy loads for several consecutive weeks, the human body will experience an automatic anticipatory rise in the production of stress hormones like adrenaline, dopamine, and cortisol, even before you touch the barbell on the competition platform. As a result, the body will then experience an increased sympathetic nervous system response.

You only want these types of chemical reactions on the day of the competition, not in the last few days leading up to the competition. Your goal should be to stimulate your parasympathetic nervous system to fully aid recovery and adaptation. This allows a super-compensation effect which will better enable you to display your true 1RM when it counts. Remember, by focusing on relaxation techniques in the final taper, you will become more sensitive to all important stress hormones which will enable you to lift more.

Never, EVER, train to complete failure in a peaking phase

Training to failure will only negatively impact the nervous system, which will also psychologically destroy your morale during the realisation phase. So do not get caught up with all the fitness bunnies rolling around on the floor pretending that they train so hard that they cannot stand up. If you train that hard, then chances are, you fucked up and will need to recover fully before you can have any hope of another good training session that week. That is pretty dumb if you have a new Personal Best to achieve.

Maybe this is just my opinion as a coach, but I train athletes to be both psychologically and physically strong. It is the whole package that wins the medal. One does not happen without the other, so you will never see any of my athletes rolling on the floor acting silly. At the very worst, they might take a knee or sit with their heads between their knees while out of the way of other lifters as a means of showing respect. I build warriors, warriors who lift weights and fight battles, and all of my lifters eventually become true warriors in life as well as in competitions. Most importantly, warriors do not wallow in weakness and self-pity. All true warriors always respect themselves and others, regardless of how much weight they can lift in any gym or competition.

11

6-WEEK 1RM METHOD

If you have been lifting more than 5 reps at less than 85% of your estimated 1RM during the previous mesocycle/phase/block, then you will need to follow the 6-Week 1RM Method approach for the full transmutation of strength developed in your previous blocks to take place.

This is a very straightforward and easy system to follow. If you are doing the six-week prep, then this is how it works:

- The training frequency per week consists of four training sessions:
  - o 1 x lower body/max effort day, alternated between single set predictor lift weeks and decreasing volume weeks
  - o 1 x upper body/dynamic effort day, which includes hypertrophy bench
  - o 1 x lower body/dynamic effort day, which includes hypertrophy squat
  - o 1 x upper body/max effort day, alternated between single set predictor lift weeks and decreasing volume weeks

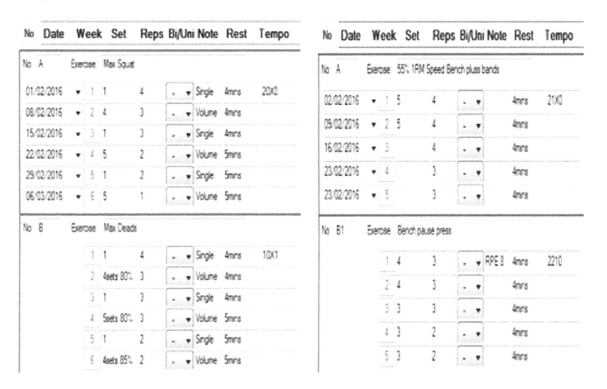

No	Date	Week	Set	Reps	Bi/Uni	Note	Rest	Tempo
No A		Exercise	Max Squat					
	01/02/2016	1	1	4	-	Single	4mns	20X0
	08/02/2016	2	4	3	-	Volume	4mns	
	15/02/2016	3	1	3	-	Single	4mns	
	22/02/2016	4	5	2	-	Volume	5mns	
	29/02/2016	5	1	2	-	Single	5mns	
	06/03/2016	6	5	1	-	Volume	5mns	
No B		Exercise	Max Deads					
		1	1	4	-	Single	4mns	10X1
		2	4sets 80%	3	-	Volume	4mns	
		3	1	3	-	Single	4mns	
		4	5sets 80%	3	-	Volume	5mns	
		5	1	2	-	Single	5mns	
		6	4sets 85%	2	-	Volume	5mns	

No	Date	Week	Set	Reps	Bi/Uni	Note	Rest	Tempo
No A		Exercise	55% 1RM Speed Bench pluss bands					
	02/02/2016	1	5	4	-		4mns	21X0
	09/02/2016	2	5	4	-		4mns	
	16/02/2016	3		4	-		4mns	
	23/02/2016	4		3	-		4mns	
	23/02/2016	5		3	-		4mns	
No B1		Exercise	Bench pause press					
		1	4	3	-	RPE 8	4mns	2210
		2	4	3	-		4mns	
		3	3	3	-		4mns	
		4	3	2	-		4mns	
		5	3	2	-		4mns	

No	Date	Week	Set	Reps	Bi/Uni	Note	Rest	Tempo
No: A	Exercise: Box Squat plus Red Bands 55%							
04/02/2016	1	4	3-4	-			4mns	21X0
11/02/2016	2	4	3-4	-			4mns	21X0
18/02/2016	3	4	3-4	-			4mns	21X0
25/02/2016	4	4	3-4	-			4mns	21X0
03/03/2016	5	4	3-4	-			4mns	21X0
No: B	Exercise: Squat pause							
	1	4	2-3	-	RPE 8		4mns	21X0
	2	4	2-3	-			4mns	21X0
	3	4	2-3	-			4mns	21X0
	4	4	2-3	-			4mns	21X0
	5	4	2-3	-			4mns	21X0

No	Date	Week	Set	Reps	Bi/Uni	Note	Rest	Tempo
No A	Exercise Max Bench							
05/02/2016	1	1	4	-	Single		4mns	21X0
12/02/2016	2	4	3	-	Volume		4mns	
19/02/2016	3	1	3	-	Single		4mns	
26/02/2016	4	5	2	-	Volume		5mns	
04/03/2016	5	1	2	-	Single		5mns	
08/03/2016	6	5	1	-	Volume		5mns	
No B1	Exercise high Board press							
	1	4	3-4	-	RPE 8-9		4mns	21X0
	2	4	3-4	-			4mns	
	3	4	3-4	-			4mns	
	4	4	2-3	-			5mns	
	5	4	2-3	-			5mns	
	6	4	2-3	-			5mns	

The volume in max effort days changes each week. These sessions should also include some accessory exercises and possibly a small amount of assistance work if needed.

The frequency remains the same until the last week. Then on the last week, you simply drop the dynamic effort days, further decreasing the volume. You will then only perform the two max effort sessions on the last week, one lower body and one upper body.

You will squat and deadlift on the same lower body day, which is specific to the sport, as you will need to know what level of fatigue the squat will create to maximise your 1RM capabilities on the deadlift. Normally, lifters in competitions get a few hours between the squat and the deadlift, but there is no guarantee. So be prepared and know what you can handle in case the break between your squats and deadlifts is shorter than expected.

- You will perform the bench separately, which is not specific to the sport of powerlifting. However, performing the squat first will not create any real fatigue for the bench so they do not need to be trained on the same day as the squat and deadlift. In addition, because the bench movements target smaller muscle groups than the squat and deadlift, you essentially recover much faster. Subsequently, when programming for the final week leading up to the championship, bench press should be performed closer to the competition day compared to the squat and deadlift to avoid premature super-compensation.
- If you are transitioning off of the back of a high-intensity high-frequency (HIHF) system or any type of system where you are squatting or benching more than twice a week, then I recommend adding some more volume to your dynamic squat and bench sessions when performing the 6-Week Phase of the 1RM Method. 3–4 sets of 3–4 reps at 70–75% of your 1RM will do the job. This is important because your body will already be accustomed to much more volume and you do not want to taper prematurely.

When adding extra volume to a dynamic session, it is essential to train *under* 80% of your estimated 1RM to ensure not to over-emphasise the nervous system involvement and subsequently, temporarily impair the necessary recovery which would negatively affect your next max effort session.

In general, I recommend training between 70–75% of your 1RM and for no more than 3–4 reps. The reason that you should rarely exceed four reps during the peaking phase is because you might accidentally begin to "train out" the correct motor pattern that you are working so incredibly hard to maintain. By training with higher reps during a peaking phase, you start to recruit more slow-twitch muscle fibre while simultaneously corrupting your body's ability to recruit from those crucial high-threshold motor units, which are so very responsible for achieving an optimum 1RM.

Another issue with training at lower percentages with higher rep ranges to increase volume is that this often over stimulates slow twitch muscle fibres during the peaking phase for optimal 1RM. You essentially do not want any possibility of fast twitch fibres being converted to more oxidative muscle fibres. Nor do you want to confuse motor unit recruitment and in turn, possibly corrupt the correct motor pattern, which is essential for achieving your ultimate 1RM.

So, when adding extra volume, I recommend training between 70–75% at maximum speed with only 3–4 reps. This system will still recruit fast twitch muscle fibre while not overly taxing the nervous system, allowing you to be fully prepared for your all-important max effort sessions.

11.1 QUICK START

- During the first week of the 6-Week realisation phase, you need to perform only 1 set at 4RM. In some ways, this is one of the most important week of the entire 6-Week 1RM Method because you really need to focus on getting it right when building up to your correct 4RM. This important step in the system defines the correct load for next week and for future weeks to follow. You do not want to build up too slowly in the warm up and risk pre-fatiguing yourself because this will lead to you being unable will to perform your true 4RM. Lastly do not increase loads between warm up attempts that are too large to allow your neuromuscular system ideal priming between attempts, this could possibly overshoot your 4RM.

I cannot stress this next point strongly enough. When performing the 1RM Method, *TECHNIQUE IS KING!* Proper technique is the only way that you can be sure that your max and volume effort weeks will truly transfer over to your best possible 1RM.

Week 1 of the 6 week 1RM Method, Single Set 4RM predictor lift performed on Squat Bench and Deadlift

- The first microcycle of the 6-Week realisation phase is a max effort 4 rep predictor lift. Again, this lift needs to be a technically-sound 4RM. The fourth rep might get a little ugly or can even be a bit of a grind, but this should definitely not occur on the second or third rep. All four reps must be technically-sound because the ultimate goal is to hit a technically-sound new Personal Best 4RM.

Example of training frequency, sets, reps and percentages in week 1:

Monday: Single set max effort 4-rep predictor lift performed on squat and deadlift only. (A) Exercise – max effort squat 86–90% 1RM 1 x 4 reps. (B) Exercise – max effort deadlift 86–90% 1RM 1 x 4 reps, plus assistant and accessory exercises.

Tuesday: (A) Exercise – dynamic bench 50–55% 1RM 4 x 3–4 reps. (B) Exercise – hypertrophy bench 4 x 3–4 reps 70–75%, plus assistant and accessory exercises.

Wednesday: Off.

Thursday: (A) Exercise – dynamic squat 50–55% 1RM 4 x 3–4 reps. (B) Exercise – dynamic deadlift 50–55% 1RM 4 x 3 – 4 reps, plus assistant and accessory exercises.

Friday: Single set max effort 4-rep predictor lift performed on the bench only. (A) Exercise – max effort bench 86–90% 1RM 1 x 4 reps, plus assistant and accessory exercises.

No	Date	Week	Set	Reps	Bi/Uni	Note	Rest	Tempo
No: A	Exercise: Max Squat							
	01/02/2016	1	1	4	-	Single	4mins	20X0
	08/02/2016	2	4	3	-	Volume	4mins	
	15/02/2016	3	1	3	-	Single	4mins	
	22/02/2016	4	5	2	-	Volume	5mins	
	29/02/2016	5	1	2	-	Single	5mins	
	06/03/2016	6	5	1	-	Volume	5mins	
No: B	Exercise: Max Deads							
		1	1	4	-	Single	4mins	10X1
		2	4sets 80%	3	-	Volume	4mins	
		3	1	3	-	Single	4mins	
		4	5sets 80%	3	-	Volume	5mins	
		5	1	2	-	Single	5mins	
		6	4sets 85%	2	-	Volume	5mins	
No: C	Exercise: High Rack pull							
		1	2	3	-	RPE 8-9	5mins	2011
		2	2	3	-		5mins	
		3	2	3	-		5mins	
		4	2	2	-		5mins	
		5	2	2	-		5mins	
		6	2	2	-		5mins	

No	Date	Week	Set	Reps	Bi/Uni	Note	Rest	Tempo
No: A	Exercise: 55% 1RM Speed Bench pluss bands							
	02/02/2016	1	5	4	-		4mins	21X0
	09/02/2016	2	5	4	-		4mins	
	16/02/2016	3		4	-		4mins	
	23/02/2016	4		3	-		4mins	
	23/02/2016	5		3	-		4mins	
No: B1	Exercise: Bench pause press							
		1	4	3	-	RPE 8	4mins	2210
		2	4	3	-		4mins	
		3	3	3	-		4mins	
		4	3	2	-		4mins	
		5	3	2	-		4mins	
No: C1	Exercise: Supenated pull ups + KG							
		1	4	5-7	-	RPE 8-9	3mins	2010
		2	4	5-7	-		3mins	
		3	4	5-7	-		3mins	
		4	4	5-7	-		3mins	
		5	4	5-7	-		3mins	
No: C2	Exercise: Half shoulder press							
		1	3	3-5	-	RPE 8-9	90mins	3010
		2	3	3-5	-		90mins	
		3	3	3-5	-		90mins	
		4	3	3-5	-		90mins	
		5	3	3-5	-		90mins	

Week 2 of the 6 week 1RM Method, Volume Triple performed on only the Squat and Bench

The second week, or the second microcycle, is a volume triple week. Simply drop one rep from your 4RM predictor lift and perform four sets of three reps on the squat and bench only. For example, if your 4RM is 400 lbs, then you will now perform only three reps of 400 lbs for 4 sets. Your goal is to execute between 10–12 reps with a minimum total volume of 10 reps. If you have a technically-sound max predictor lift and are still struggling to perform all four sets of three reps, then go ahead and drop a single rep from the last few sets to perform only 2 reps if needed. Example:

If you are struggling to achieve the recommended volume of reps prescribed, please see the example below:

- Set #1: 3 reps
- Set #2: 3 reps

No	Date	Week	Set	Reps	Bi/Uni	Note	Rest	Tempo

No: A — Exercise: Box Squat plus Red Bands 55%

No	Date	Week	Set	Reps	Bi/Uni	Note	Rest	Tempo
	04/02/2016	1	4	3-4	-		4mins	21X0
	11/02/2016	2	4	3-4	-		4mins	21X0
	18/02/2016	3	4	3-4	-		4mins	21X0
	25/02/2016	4	4	3-4	-		4mins	21X0
	03/03/2016	5	4	3-4	-		4mins	21X0

No: B — Exercise: Squat pause

Week	Set	Reps	Bi/Uni	Note	Rest	Tempo
1	4	2-3	-	RPE 8	4mins	21X0
2	4	2-3	-		4mins	21X0
3	4	2-3	-		4mins	21X0
4	4	2-3	-		4mins	21X0
5	4	2-3	-		4mins	21X0

No: C — Exercise: Dynamic Deadlift plus red bands

Week	Set	Reps	Bi/Uni	Note	Rest	Tempo
1	4	3-4	-		4mins	3010
2	4	3-4	-		4mins	3010
3	4	3-4	-		4mins	3010
4	4	3-4	-		4mins	3010
5	4	3-4	-		4mins	3010

No: D — Exercise: Hack squat

Week	Set	Reps	Bi/Uni	Note	Rest	Tempo
1	3	5-7	-	RPE 7-8	3mins	3010
2	3	5-7	-		3mins	3010
3	3	5-7	-		3mins	3010
4	3	5-7	-		3mins	3010
5	3	5-7	-		3mins	3010

No: A — Exercise: Max Bench

No	Date	Week	Set	Reps	Bi/Uni	Note	Rest	Tempo
	05/02/2016	1	1	4	-	Single	4mins	21X0
	12/02/2016	2	4	3	-	Volume	4mins	
	19/02/2016	3	1	3	-	Single	4mins	
	26/02/2016	4	5	2	-	Volume	5mins	
	04/03/2016	5	1	2	-	Single	5mins	
	08/03/2016	6	5	1	-	Volume	5mins	

No: B1 — Exercise: high Board press

Week	Set	Reps	Bi/Uni	Note	Rest	Tempo
1	4	3-4	-	RPE 8-9	4mins	21X0
2	4	3-4	-		4mins	
3	4	3-4	-		4mins	
4	4	2-3	-		5mins	
5	4	2-3	-		5mins	
6	4	2-3	-		5mins	

No: B2 — Exercise: Strate Arm pos flys

Week	Set	Reps	Bi/Uni	Note	Rest	Tempo
1	3	5-7	-	RPE 7	3mins	3010
2	3	5-7	-		3mins	3010
3	3	5-7	-		3mins	3010
4	3	5-7	-		3mins	3010
5	3	5-7	-		3mins	3010
6	3	5-7	-		3mins	3010

No: C1 — Exercise: B/B Tricep ext

Week	Set	Reps	Bi/Uni	Note	Rest	Tempo
1	3	5-7	-	RPE 7	90sec	2010
2	3	5-7	-		90sec	2010
3	3	5-7	-		90sec	2010
4	3	5-7	-		90sec	2010
5	3	5-7	-		90sec	2010
6	3	5-7	-		90sec	2010

No: C2 — Exercise: Inverted pull ups supine grip

Week	Set	Reps	Bi/Uni	Note	Rest	Tempo
1	3	3-5	-	RPE 8	90sec	2011
2	3	3-5	-		90sec	2011
3	3	3-5	-		90sec	2011
4	3	3-5	-		90sec	2011
5	3	3-5	-		90sec	2011
6	3	3-5	-		90sec	2011

- Set #3: 3 reps
- Set #4: 2 reps (achieving one less rep)
- Total reps achieving over the minimum volume threshold of 11 reps total

Important information: You will notice that I do not mention deadlift on the volume triple week. That is because after performing 4 sets of volume triple on the squat at anywhere between 86–90% 1RM you will never be able to perform quality sets of deadlift at a similar intensity.

For this reason, you simply perform 4 sets of deadlifts at 80% for triples, this allows you to maintain good form and not over stress your neuromuscular system so you are able to recover optimally for your next all important max effort predictor lift on the squat and deadlift.

Example of training frequency, sets, reps and percentages in week 2:

Monday: (A) Exercise – volume triples squat 86–90% 1RM 4 x 3 reps. (B) Exercise – deadlift will be performed at 80% 1RM 4 x 3 reps, plus assistant and accessory exercises.

Tuesday: (A) Exercise – dynamic bench 50–55% 1RM 4 x 3–4 reps. (B) Exercise – hypertrophy bench 4 x 3–4 reps 70–75%, plus assistant and accessory exercises.

Wednesday: Off.

Thursday: (A) Exercise – dynamic squat 50–55% 1RM 4 x 3–4 reps. (B) Exercise – dynamic deadlift 50–55% 1RM 4 x 3–4 reps, plus assistant and accessory exercises.

Friday: (A) Exercise – volume triples bench 86–90% 1RM 4 x 3 reps, plus assistant and accessory exercises.

Remember, we all get sick or have a bad day from time to time. So even if you cannot achieve the minimum amount of volume of 11 reps, it is far more important to perform high-quality technically-sound reps than achieving the desired volume threshold.

One thing you should never do is add another set to the volume weeks if you have already achieved minimum volume required. This can negatively affect your nervous system's recovery for next week's max triple session.

Week 3 of the 6 week 1RM Method, Single Set Max Triple performed on Squat, Bench and Deadlift

- The third microcycle of a 6-Week realisation phase is a max triple predictor lift. The weight should be roughly the same weight that you expect to use on your first attempt on the day of competition. Again, this lift needs to be a technically-sound triple. The third rep might get a little ugly or can even be a bit of a grind, but this should definitely not occur on the first or second rep. All three reps must be technically-sound because the ultimate goal is to hit a technically-sound new Personal Best max triple.

Example of training frequency, sets, reps and percentages in week 3:

Monday: Single set max effort triple predictor lift performed only on squat and deadlift. (A) Exercise – max effort triple squat 90–94% 1RM 1 x 3 reps (B) Exercise – max effort triple deadlift 90–94% 1 x 3 reps, plus assistant and accessory exercises.

Tuesday: (A) Exercise – dynamic bench 50–55% 1RM 4 x 3–4 reps (B) Exercise – hypertrophy bench 4 x 3–4 reps 70–75%, plus assistant and accessory exercises.

Wednesday: Off.

Thursday: (A) Exercise – dynamic squat 50–55% 1RM 4 x 3–4 reps (B) Exercise – dynamic deadlift 50–55% 1RM 4 x 3–4 reps, plus assistant and accessory exercises.

Friday: Single set max effort triple predictor lift performed only on the bench. (A) Exercise – max effort bench 90–94% 1RM 1 x 2 reps, plus assistant and accessory exercises.

Week 4 of the 6 week 1RM Method, **Volume Double performed on only the Squat and Bench**

- The fourth week is the second volume week. The volume serves to cement-in your improving maximal strength level. Once again, you will drop one rep from your predictor lift, but this time, you will perform five sets of two reps. All things being equal concerning sleep, nutrition, stress levels, etc., this should be a tough but realistic session to execute successfully. If your technique is breaking down by the fourth set, then simply drop the last set completely or just perform one or two singles. In the volume double week, you are striving to execute a volume of 10 reps. With a minimum total volume of 8 reps to be achieved, this way you will still hit minimum volume threshold for maximal strength realisation to occur.

Important Information: You will that notice I do not mention deadlift on the volume double week. This is because after performing 5 sets of doubles on the squat at anywhere between 90–94% you will never be able to perform quality sets of deadlift at a similar intensity.

For this reason, you simply perform 4 sets of deadlifts at 80% for triples. This allows you to maintain good form without over stressing your neuromuscular system, enabling you to recover optimally for your next all important max effort predictor lift on the squat and deadlift.

Example of training frequency, sets, reps and percentages in week 4:

Monday: (A) Exercise – volume doubles squat 90–94% 1RM 5 x 2 reps. (B) Exercise – deadlift will be performed at 80% 1RM 4 x 3 reps, plus assistant and accessory exercises.

Tuesday: (A) Exercise – dynamic bench 50–55% 1RM 4 x 3–4 reps. (B) Exercise – hypertrophy bench 4 x 3–4 reps 70–75%, plus assistant and accessory exercises.

Wednesday: Off.

Thursday: (A) Exercise – dynamic squat 50–55% 1RM 4 x 3–4 reps. (B) Exercise – dynamic deadlift 50–55% 1RM 4 x 3–4 reps, plus assistant and accessory exercises.

Friday: (A) Exercise – volume doubles bench 90–94% 1RM 5 x 2 reps, plus assistant and accessory exercises.

As I stated for last week's instructions, we all get sick or have a bad day from time to time. So, even if you cannot achieve the minimum amount of volume, it is far more important to perform high-quality, technically-sound reps than to achieve your minimum volume threshold.

One thing you should never do is add another set to the volume weeks because this can negatively affect your central nervous system's recovery for next week's max double session.

Week 5 of the 6 week 1RM Method, Single Set Max Double performed on Squat Bench and Deadlift.

- During the fifth week, you perform your max double. The weight should be roughly the same weight that you expect to use on your second attempt on the day of competition. Again, this lift needs to be a technically-sound double. When executing this load at a competition as your second attempt, it will build a good total and give you all of the accurate feedback needed to make the right decision for establishing your true 1RM for the day of the championship.

Example of training frequency, sets, reps and percentages in week 5:

Monday: Single set max effort double predictor lift performed only on squat and deadlift. (A) Exercise – max effort double squat 94–97% 1RM 1 x 2 reps (B) Exercise – max effort double deadlift 94–97% 1 x 2 reps, plus assistant and accessory exercises.

Tuesday: (A) Exercise – dynamic bench 50–55% 1RM 4 x 3–4 reps (B) Exercise – hypertrophy bench 4 x 3–4 reps 70–75%, plus assistant and accessory exercises.

Wednesday: Off.

Thursday: (A) Exercise – dynamic squat 50–55% 1RM 4 x 3–4 reps (B) Exercise – dynamic deadlift 50–55% 1RM 4 x 3–4 reps, plus assistant and accessory exercises.

Friday: Single set max effort double predictor lift performed only on the bench. (A) Exercise – max effort bench 94–97% 1RM 1 x 2 reps, plus assistant and accessory exercises.

WEEK 6 (FINAL WEEK) of the 6 week 1RM Method, Volume Singles performed on only the Squat and Bench

- The sixth and final microcycle is a volume single week. Perform 4–5 sets of singles using your max double load. Week 6 is an excellent time to pull together all of the technical and psychological aspects for your lifts. Even performing the lifting movements under commands can be of great benefit to all lifters from novices, all the way up to World Class Champions. Remember, technique is always paramount! If you start grinding on the third or fourth set of this final week, then it is likely time to throw in the towel and call it a day!

Important Information: You will notice that I do not mention deadlift on the volume single week. This is because after performing 5 sets of singles on the squat, at anywhere between 94–97% you will be unable to perform quality sets of deadlift at similar intensity.

For this reason, you simply perform 3–4 sets of deadlifts at 85% for doubles. This allows you to maintain good form, without over stressing your neuromuscular system and therefore, enabling you to recover optimally for the championship.

Example of training frequency, sets, reps and percentages in week 6:

Monday: (A) Exercise – volume singles squat 94–97% 1RM 5 x 1 rep (B) Exercise – deadlift performed at 85% 1RM 4 x 2 reps, plus only a small amount of accessory exercises if needed.

Tuesday: (A) Exercise – volume singles bench 94–97% 1RM 5 x 1 rep, plus only a small amount of assistant and accessory exercises if needed.

Wednesday: Off.

Thursday: Off.

Friday: Off.

Saturday: Off.

Sunday: Championships

As you can see, this monthly plan (mesocycle) allows 6 days of full recovery between squats and deadlifts and 5 days of full recovery between bench. The mesocycle outlined above will generally better suit intermediate competitors. Novices lifting lower loads will generally benefit from fewer recovery days in the final microcycle,

MON	TUE	WED	THU	FRI	SAT	SUN
1x4 Max Four squat & Deadlift, Assisant & accessory work	Dynamic Bench, 2 Assistant & accessory work	3	Dynamic Squat, 4 Assistant & accessory work	1x4 Max Four bench, 5 Assistant & accessory work	6	7
4x3 Volume triple squat, 4x3 deadlift 80% Assistant & accessory	Dynamic Bench, 9 Assistant & accessory work	10	Dynamic Squat, 11 Assistant & accessory work	4x3 Volume triple bench, 12 Assistant & accessory work	13	14
1x3 Max triple squat & Deadlift, 15 Assisant & accessory work	Dynamic Bench, 16 Assistant & accessory work	17	Dynamic Squat, 18 Assistant & accessory work	1x3 Max triple bench, 19 Assistant & accessory work	20	21
5x2 Volume double squat, 5x3 Deadlift triples 80% Assisant &	Dynamic Bench, 23 Assistant & accessory	24	Dynamic Squat, 25 Assistant & accessory	5x2 Volume double bench, 26 Assistant & accessory	27	28
1x2 Max double squat & Deadlift, 29 Assisant & accessory work	Dynamic Bench, 1 Assistant & accessory work	2	Dynamic Squat, 3 Assistant & accessory work	1x2 Max double bench, 4 Assistant & accessory work	5	6
5x1 Volume single squat, 5x2 Deadlift doubles 85% Assisant & accessory	5x1 Volume single bench Assistant & accessory work	9	10	11	12	13 Meet

whereas advanced competitors lifting very large loads may benefit from adding more recovery days in the final microcycle.

Please refer to the training frequency section for more detailed information on how to organise the last month of training (mesocycle) for effective peaking.

Ideal minimum volume is between 4–5 reps, but as I mentioned before, it is important to remember that we all get sick or have a bad day from time to time. So even if you cannot achieve the minimum amount of volume, it is far more important to perform high-quality, technically-sound reps than to achieve your minimum volume threshold. Remember if you start grinding out reps, listen to your body, it is time to stop, call it a day and save yourself for the championships.

11.2 Complete 6 Week 1RM Method

If you have been performing under 85% of your estimated 1RM on the key lifts you wish to peak, then you should begin by performing the 6 week 1RM Method. Perform one set of a max effort four rep predictor lift on the squat bench and deadlift.

<u>OVERVIEW</u> of the 6 week 1RM Method

Start with a single set Max Effort Predictor Lift of 4-reps on all the lifts you hope to peak for a 1RM attempt.

You should also always perform the 6 week 1RM Method if you have been separating squats and deadlifts into different training days. This is regardless of if you have been training above or below your 85% estimated

1RM. This is because you will need to start to place both squat and deadlift within the same workout. It is important to start tailoring your training sessions so that they are specific to the sport of powerlifting.

The only lifters I get to perform squats and deadlifts on different days are novice lifters who are not yet ready to compete, or occasionally lifters who I am trying to re-pattern a new motor pattern on their deadlifts and do not want fatigue to interfere with their ability to learn or re-learn the ideal technique. I will also sometimes separate these two lifts if the deadlift is lagging behind the squat to help bring up strength levels on this lift, but I would only program for this in a general preparation phase. In any event, these lifters will not be ready to go into a competition off the back of these types of methods. The reason you place both the squat and deadlift in the same training session is because performing both of these on the same day is specific to the sport of powerlifting and therefore, this is sport specific training.

During competition, squats, bench and deadlifts are performed on the same day in this order, so lifters should get used to performing the deadlift post squat for the training to be truly specific. This will better the chances of a positive outcome at a championship. It is important the lifters become accustomed to performing technically sound deadlifting post squat in a peaking phase, even if the squat has created some fatigue, as this is specific to the sport. Remember the higher the level you compete at the less time you will generally have between squat and deadlift events.

In the most extreme case I have coached a lifter at the IPF World championships where we had a little under an hour between the squat and the deadlift to get back out on the platform and perform his first deadlift attempt. That might not sound too bad, but when you consider 15-mins warm up for bench, 30-mins for all three flights on bench and then only 15-mins to warm up on deadlift to 290kg, this is clearly not very long and you will incur considerable fatigue. This however, is not the norm, but you can start to see the importance of training squats and deadlifts on the same day. To further highlight it is importance, the incredible lifter Stephen 'the Screamer' Manual would have been unaccustomed to post squat fatigue had he not been training both squats and deadlifts on the same day and therefore, would not have been able to deadlift to the same level as he did at the 2015 IPF World championships ultimately, won him the Bronze Medal.

2016 EPF European championships, 93kg Pierre Shillingford deadlifting 302.5kg

<u>Week 1</u> of the 6 week 1RM Method, single 4RM predictor lift performed on Squat, Bench and Deadlift

When executing the single set Max Effort 4 rep Predictor Lift, always focus on performing high-quality reps with proper technique. The only rep in this max effort single set that could or should be a bit of a grind will be the final, fourth rep. If you are grinding out your first or second rep, then you will never achieve the maximum positive effects for adaptation during the volume triple week.

If your attempt selection is incorrect and you are grinding out badly and do not think you can successfully get your second or third rep, simply rack the bar, rest 6–8 mins and then drop the weight on the bar by 3–5%. If you are grinding out on your second rep, drop the weight by 5% and if you are grinding out on your third rep, drop the weight by 2.5%. If you were roughly lifting 5% less in your last warm up set, then rack the bar and simply take this number as your max effort 4 rep predictor lift. It is very important to note that you only have **one** second shot at getting the attempt selection right. Do not ever attempt to try more than two max effort attempts on predictor lift week as this will create too much volume to recover from positively. Sometimes you will find as long as you did not grind out to badly and create energy leaks, your reduced second attempt at a predictor lift will go incredibly well and this is more than likely because of the post-activation potentiation effect from the previous set. If you honestly do not think you have another attempt in you, simply subtract 5% and call this your 4 rep max. It is important to try not to make these same mistakes again during the coming single set Max Triple Predictor Lift week as your goal is to try and get each attempt selection spot on. Getting attempt selection spot on in training will help you to become better at attempt selection on the all-important competition day. It is important to adhere to the protocols of the 1RM Method as strictly as possible, right from the very beginning.

<u>Week 2</u> of the 6 week 1RM Method, volume triple performed on only the Squat and Bench

Take the weight you performed on your Max 4 rep Predictor Lift and perform 4 sets of triples on the Squat and Bench in this volume week.

On this the second week of the 6 week 1RM Method it is important to note you will not be performing deadlifts at the same load as you did in the previous week on the single set max effort 4 rep predictor lift. This is because although it is important to get used to handling some fatigue from the single set predictor lifts for your training to be sport specific, it will be practically impossible and a bad idea, to lift large loads post volume triple squats. Deadlifting with the same loads as week one after the 4 sets of squat triples would not be specific to the sport of powerlifting as you will never normally be exposed to such a large level of volume and fatigue before attempting a 1RM deadlift in a championship. If you are foolish enough to try and perform heavy deadlifts, post volume squat, you are likely to train with poor technique, and may even start to train out a good motor pattern. You may even create so much cumulative fatigue that you negatively affect your CNS, making you unable to perform the all-important single set max effort double predictor lift in the following weeks training.

<u>IMPORT INFORMATION</u> – only perform 80% of your estimated 1RM deadlift for 3 sets of 3 reps in week 2

In week 2, volume double squats and bench, simply take the weight you performed on your max effort 4 rep predictor lift on squat and bench, drop 1 rep and perform 4 sets of triples with this weight in this volume week.

During the execution of the volume triple week, you should never experience a bad first or second set. Things might begin to get tough around the end of the third set, but the fourth set is when you should start really feeling the effects. If, however, something happens and you begin experiencing bad sets earlier than expected, then this is normally a sign of perhaps an oncoming cold or flu, lack of quality sleep, lack of adequate nutrition, or very high stress levels resulting from your daily life. The only other reason this can happen is if you are performing technically poor lifts or low-quality reps on your max effort predictor lift.

This is why it is always a big mistake to be grinding out your third rep when performing your max effort 4 rep predictor lift during the 1RM Method, as the weight in the following volume triples week will be too heavy to achieve positive adaptation. Meanwhile, trying to grind out four sets of volume triples at this load will only have extremely negative impacts on the strength adaptation and peaking that should be taking place.

So, let's say that you make one of these mistakes and your second or third sets are a real grind. Simply drop one rep off of each set you have left and perform quality doubles instead. Then, if needed, simply add-on another set, thereby performing a total of five sets instead of the recommended four. By making this small modification you still achieve the minimum threshold volume of between 10–12 reps.

There may come a time when you cut reps from triples to doubles and are still grinding reps out badly so you think you might need to cut even more than one set to achieve good quality. If this happens, then you should probably just cut your losses and simply drop the weight by 2.5% so that you can perform a quality technique for reps at RPE 8–9, striving for a minimum total volume of 10–12 reps. Then next week, focus on performing a better quality single set max triple at RPE 9–10 while trying not to make the same mistakes.

Remember, the minimum volume threshold in this volume week is, 10–12 reps at between 86–90% of your 1RM. Good quality reps are more important than volume, so it is better to cut sets even if you probably will not achieve minimum volume threshold.

Week 3 of the 6 week 1RM Method, single set max triple predictor lift performed on Squat, Bench and Deadlift.

If you have been performing over 85% of your estimated 1RM you should begin by performing the 4 week 1RM Method, starting with a single set Max Effort Triple Predictor Lift.

When executing the single set Max Effort Triple Predictor Lift week, always focus on performing high-quality reps with proper technique. The only rep in this max effort single set that could or should be a bit of a grind will be the final, third rep. If you are grinding out your first, then you will never achieve the maximum positive effects for adaptation during the volume double week.

If your attempt selection is incorrect and you are grinding out badly and do not think you can successfully get your second rep, simply rack the bar, rest 6–8mins and then drop the weight on the bar by 3–5%. If you are grinding out on your second rep and do not think you can get the third rep, then follow the same steps and drop the weight by 3%. If you were roughly lifting 5% less in your last warm up set, then rack the bar and simply take this number as your max triple predictor lift. It is important to note you only have **one** second shot at getting attempt selection right. Do not ever attempt to try more than two max effort attempts on a predictor lift week as this will create too much volume from which to recover positively. Sometimes you will find that as long as you did not grind out badly and create energy leaks, your second attempt at a predictor lift will go incredibly well, this is more than likely because of the post activation potentiation effect from the previous set. If you honestly do not think you have another attempt in you, then simply subtract 5% and call this your max effort triple predictor lift. It is important to try not to make these same mistakes again during the coming single Set Max Double Predictor Lift week, as your goal is to try and get each attempt selection spot on. Getting attempt selection spot on in training will help to become better at attempt selection on the all-important competition day. It is important to adhere to the protocols of the 1RM Method as strictly as possible, right from the very beginning.

Week 4 of the 6 week 1RM Method, volume doubles performed on only the Squat and Bench

Take the weight you performed on your Max Triple Predictor Lift and perform 5 sets of doubles on the Squat and Bench in this volume week.

On this the fourth week of the 6 week 1RM Method it is important to note you will not be performing deadlifts at the same load as you did in the previous week on the single set max effort triple predictor lift. This is because, although it is important to get used to handling some fatigue from the single set predictor lifts for your training to be sport specific, it will be practically impossible and a bad idea, to lift large loads post volume double squats. Deadlifting with the same loads as week three after the 5 sets of squat doubles would not be specific to the sport of powerlifting as you will never normally be exposed to such a large level of volume and fatigue before attempting a 1RM deadlift in a championship. If you are foolish enough to try and perform heavy deadlifts, post volume squat, you are likely to train with poor technique, and may even start to train out a good motor pattern. You may even create so much cumulative fatigue that you negatively affect your CNS, making you unable to perform the all-important single set max effort double predictor lift in the following weeks training.

IMPORT INFORMATION – only perform 80% of your estimated 1RM deadlift for 4 sets of 3 reps in week 4

In week 4, volume double squats and bench, simply take the weight you performed on your max effort triple predictor lift on Squat and Bench, drop 1 rep and perform 5 sets of doubles with this weight in this volume week.

During the execution of the volume double week, you should never experience a bad first or second set. Things might begin to get tough around the end of the fourth set, but the fifth set is when you should start really feeling the effects. If, however, something happens and you begin experiencing bad sets earlier than expected, then this is normally a sign of perhaps an oncoming cold or flu, lack of quality sleep, lack of adequate nutrition, or very high stress levels resulting from your daily life. The only other reason this can happen is if you are performing technically poor lifts or low-quality reps on your max effort predictor lift.

This is why it is always a big mistake to be grinding out your reps when performing your predictor lift during the 1RM Method, as the weight in the following volume doubles week will be too heavy to achieve positive adaptation. Meanwhile, trying to grind out five sets of volume doubles at this load will only have extremely negative impacts on the strength adaptation and peaking that should be taking place.

So, let's say that you make one of these mistakes and your third or fourth sets are a real grind. Simply drop one rep off of each set that you have left and perform quality singles instead. If needed, simply add-on another set, thereby performing a total of six sets instead of the recommended five. By making this small modification you still achieve the minimum threshold volume of between 8–10 reps.

There may come a time when you cut reps from doubles to singles and still think you are grinding reps out badly and so are not achieving good quality. If this happens, then you should probably just cut your losses and simply drop the weight by 2.5% so you can perform quality technique for reps at RPE 9, striving for a minimum total volume of 8–10 reps. Then next week, focus on performing a better quality single set max double at RPE 10 while trying not to make the same mistakes.

Remember, the minimum volume threshold in this volume week is, 8–10 reps at between 90–94% of your 1RM. Good quality reps are more important than volume, so it is better to cut sets even if you probably will not achieve minimum volume threshold.

Week 5 of the 6 week 1RM Method, single set max double predictor lift performed on Squat, Bench and Deadlift.

When executing the single set Max Effort Double Predictor Lift week, always focus on performing high-quality reps with proper technique. The only rep in this max effort single set that could or should be a bit of a grind will be the final, second rep. If you are grinding out your first, then you will never achieve the maximum positive effects for adaptation during the volume single week.

If your attempt selection is incorrect and you are grinding out badly and do not think you can successfully get your second rep, simply rack the bar, rest 6–8mins and then drop the weight on the bar by 3–5%. If you were roughly lifting 5% less in your last warm up set, then rack the bar and simply take this number as your max double predictor lift. It is very important to note you only have **one** second shot at getting attempt selection right. Do not ever attempt to try more than two max effort attempts on a predictor lift week as this

will create too much volume to recover from positively. Sometimes you will find as long as you did not grind
o   u   t   b   a   d   l   y
and create energy leaks, your second attempt at a predictor lift will go incredibly well, this is more than likely because of the post activation potentiation effect from the previous set. If you honestly do not think you have another attempt in you, then simply subtract 5% and call this your max effort double predictor lift. It is important to adhere to the protocols of the 1RM Method as strictly as possible, right from the very beginning.

Once again, I must stress when executing the single set max double week, always perform high-quality reps. The only rep in the set that could or should be a bit of a grind is the second rep, or you will never achieve the maximum positive effects during the following volume single week. It is a big mistake to grind out your first rep when performing this stage of the 1RM Method, the max double week, as the weight in the following volume single week will be too heavy to achieve maximum positive adaptation. Meanwhile, attempting to grind out five sets of singles at this load will only have extremely negative impacts on strength adaptation and peaking that should take place in preparation for the championship.

WEEK 6 (THE FINAL WEEK) of the 6 week 1RM Method, volume singles performed on only the Squat and Bench

Take the weight you performed on your Max Double Predictor Lift and perform 5 sets of single reps under commands on the squat and bench only.

On this final week of the 1RM Method it is important to note, you will NOT be performing deadlifts at the same load as you did in the previous week on the single set max effort double predictor lift. This is because, although it is important to get used to handling some fatigue from the single set predictor lifts for your training to be sport specific, it will be practically impossible, and a bad idea, to lift large loads post volume double squats. Deadlifting with the same loads as week five after the 5 sets of squat singles would not be specific to the sport of powerlifting as you will never normally be exposed to such a large level of volume and fatigue before attempting a 1RM deadlift in a championship. If you are foolish enough to try and perform heavy deadlifts post volume squat, you are likely to train with poor technique and may even start to train out a good motor pattern. You may even create so much cumulative fatigue that you negatively affect your CNS, making you unable to perform your ultimate 1RM in competition.

<u>IMPORT INFORMATION</u> – only perform 85% of your estimated 1RM deadlift for 3–4 sets of good quality doubles. If you start grinding out, call it a day, regardless of sets or reps completed.

During the execution of the volume single week, you should never experience a bad first or second set. Things might begin to get tough around the third or fourth set, but the fifth set is when you should really start feeling the effects. If, however, something happens and you begin to start experiencing bad sets earlier than expected, then listen to your body and call it a day. As long as you have performed three singles under commands, you will have achieved the minimum volume effective dosage. If you have not performed a minimum of three singles before you are grinding out, then you will need to look at dropping the weight by 2.5% depending on how the lift looked. It is very important to remember in this taper week that the moment you start to grind, it is time to either call it a day, or if you have not performed at least three singles, then time to drop the weight.

Trying to grind out five sets of volume singles at this load will only have extremely negative impacts on strength adaptation and peaking that should take place.

Remember the minimum volume threshold in this volume week is 3–5 reps at between 94–97% of your 1RM. Good quality reps are more important than volume, so it is better to cut sets, even if you probably will not achieve the minimum volume threshold.

BUT REMEMBER! In this FINAL WEEK, *"less is MORE!"* **So if it gets really tough by the third or fourth set, call it a day and save your energy for the meet.**

The Final Week: Taper Week

In the final lower and upper body max effort volume sessions, you will be predominately focussing on your competition lifts. It is entirely acceptable to perform a certain amount of isolation accessory exercises that only target small muscle groups because these will not create a great deal of fatigue. Recovery from these types of exercises also occurs at a much faster rate than exercises targeting large muscle groups. Most importantly, you should also walk away from these workouts feeling like you could have done more.

Remember, this is not the time to grind out lifts or even, in some cases, perform assistance exercises. This is the time to allow the body to super-compensate if the ultimate goal is to hit a new Personal Best at the championship.

If you have lower strength levels, then you will not need as many days for your nervous system to recover fully and super-compensate.

Also, because lifters with lower strength levels tend to tax their nervous system to a far lesser degree, they are far more likely to suffer from a de-training effect more quickly. This is another reason to take less time off before a competition.

Most lifters entering a competition have spent several weeks or even months training extremely hard to boost maximal strength levels. One easy week is not going to erase all of your hard work and progress. Instead, these last few days will allow your body to fully realise and showcase all of that hard work that you have already accomplished. So trust the work that you have already put in and give your body a chance to reward you for your past efforts.

2016 EPF European championships, 66kg lifter Andrew Dawes winning the gold medal in the squat with 202.5kg

11.3 To Sum It All Up...

The 1RM Method is all about training to succeed, which is exactly what you are going to do at a competition because your goal should always be to get 9 out of 9.

If you do not have the energy or capacity to finish necessary sets, then simply walk away. There is no shame here. It is more important to be safe. This is especially true for accessory and assistance work. Never try and increase the volume on another day so that you can still attain your projected weekly volume or target. This is a *BIG MISTAKE* in any phase of training, but most especially during a peaking phase because the cumulative fatigue will negatively affect your performance in coming sessions. If you do not feel that you can do it, *do not!* It is always best to just cut your losses and have a lower volume day by dropping sets on your assistant or accessory work. Always listen to your body.

With the 1RM Method, there is a certain amount of built-in flexibility. There is nothing wrong with completely dropping certain dynamic effort sessions if you need the rest. In fact, the only sessions that you simply cannot miss under any circumstances are the max effort sessions, but obviously, the dynamic and functional hypertrophy sessions are very important too. Your body sees them, to some degree, as active recovery days.

Let's say, for some reason, you simply cannot perform the max effort predictor lift or volume session on the day you have planned due to sickness or other issues. Normally, the best thing to do in this scenario is to first drop the dynamic effort and functional hypertrophy session that was planned. This is very important in a peaking phase as it will not be possible to recover positively with under 48-hours between max effort sessions.

By scrapping the dynamic session, it will give you more flexibility to move your session within the microcycle. The key point is to preferably make sure you have at least **72-hours** between max effort lifting and at least 48-hours between performing dynamic effort and functional hypertrophy sessions.

For instance, take the following training frequency:

- **Monday** – max effort predictor lift or max effort volume session on squat and deadlift
- **Thursday** – dynamic and functional hypertrophy session on squat and deadlift

If you are unable to perform the max effort predictor lift or max effort volume session on Monday, then you would drop the Thursday session and perform the max effort session on Tuesday, Wednesday or Thursday. Tuesday or Wednesday is preferable as this would give you between 5 and 6 full days of recovery before your next max effort session on the following Monday, as opposed to only 4 to 5 days.

72-hours between max efforts sessions should be the bare minimum and with anything less it is best to skip the session completely. If this was a max effort predictor lift, you will have to just use an estimated 3RM or 2RM based on the performance of your previous lift.

Do not forget to always pay close attention to your stress levels, both specific and non-specific. Let's say that during one of the weeks of training you have a great deal of personal and work-related stress in your life. You might need to consider dropping one dynamic/hypertrophy session just to give your nervous system time to fully recover.

11.4 Troubleshooting

If you are feeling beat up and tired, the first thing to do is to consider dropping or reducing the amount of assistance and accessory exercises in your program. This is very important if you want to be successful and achieve your ideal peak and achieve your ultimate 1RM in competition. The first exercises to drop or reduce should be your assistance exercises. This is the exercise that uses similar motor patterns to the movement you are hoping to peak.

So if you are feeling mentally, physically, and emotionally drained, drop or reduce some of these exercises first to reduce the negative impact on your nervous system and achieve a better quality recovery.

Do's and Don'ts

- On the day before the competition, try not to think about lifting or the competition whatsoever. Also try to avoid conducting any sort of visualisation techniques as this will only increase your levels of sympathetic nervousness. Believe me, nothing good will come of this. Most likely, you will just experience a very restless night's sleep due to overstimulated sympathetic and under-stimulated parasympathetic nervous systems. This imbalance will only lead to feeling tired and fatigued on the crucial day of competition.
- I always tell my lifters to make sure to turn the lights off, or at least, dim them to a lower level for a good few hours before ultimately planning to fall asleep. Scientific research shows that low lighting better stimulates the pineal gland, which produces the chemical melatonin that positively affects the modulation of sleep patterns.
- I also recommend that lifters avoid trying to force themselves to go to sleep *too* early. This rarely works and is usually futile and a waste of mental energy. You will likely end up lying in bed for perhaps several hours trying to fall asleep. The better option is simply to turn the lights down low or completely off while keeping the room temperature cool (not cold) and getting into some very comfortable sleeping clothes.
- Perhaps the most important piece of advice that I can offer is to only go to bed when you actually feel tired. Remember, staying up a bit later while still achieving five or six hours of good quality sleep the night before a meet is still much better than getting a full eight or nine hours of broken, restless sleep.

If you try these useful *Do's and Don'ts* and sleep still eludes you, do not get too down on yourself. Certainly do not start thinking that tomorrow's competition is going to be a huge bust! Far too many times I have witnessed powerlifters arriving at a competition bleary-eyed after having suffered miserably on an excruciatingly long airline flight that was either previously delayed or cancelled and yet, they still managed to achieve a new Personal Best! So relax, as you have done all the hard work, it is now time to show everyone, and more importantly, yourself, just how strong you are.

From my over twenty years of experience with coaching and prepping powerlifters for competitions, missing a good night's sleep does not ultimately have that much effect on most lifters' performances. Sleep is kind of like training, in the sense that missing one session here or there will not automatically make you weak, but cumulatively it will have a tremendous negative impact on competitive performances.

After reviewing the HRV data analysis of lifters, I find that those who tend to naturally possess a more nervous disposition usually benefit greatly from staying busy in the final days leading up to a championship. In short, keeping busy makes them perform better on the day of the competition. This is probably because they are not sitting around worrying, essentially wasting loads of mental energy that is useful to win the medal. After all, worrying causes stress and my current HRV data analysis positively supports these findings.

Visualisation techniques can be extremely useful if they are performed at the appropriate times, but they can very negative if you spend way too much time every day visualising your squats technique or the competition itself. Interesting to note: If your body has been exposed to consistent heavy loads for several consecutive weeks, the human body will experience an automatic anticipatory rise in the production of stress hormones like adrenaline, dopamine, and cortisol, even before you touch the barbell on the competition platform. As a result, the body will then experience an increased sympathetic nervous system response.

You only want these types of chemical reactions on the day of the competition, not in the last few days leading up to the competition. Your goal should be on stimulating your parasympathetic nervous system to fully aid recovery and adaptation. This allows a super-compensation effect which will better enable you to display your true 1RM when it counts. Remember, by focusing on relaxation techniques in the final taper, you will become more sensitive to all important stress hormones which will enable you to lift more.

Never, EVER, train to complete failure in a peaking phase

Training to Failure will only negatively impact the nervous system, which will also psychologically destroy your morale during the realisation phase. So do not get caught up with all the fitness bunnies rolling around on the floor pretending that they train so hard that they can't stand up. If you train that hard, then chances are, you fucked up and will need to recover fully before you can have any hope of another good training session that week. That's pretty dumb if you have a new Personal Best to achieve.

Maybe this is just my opinion as a coach, but I train athletes to be both psychologically and physically strong. It is the whole package that wins the medal. One does not happen without the other, so you will never see any of my athletes rolling on the floor acting silly. At the very worst, they might take a knee or sit with their heads between their knees while out of the way of other lifters as a means of showing respect. I build warriors, warriors who lift weights and fight battles, and all of my lifters eventually become true warriors in life as well as in competitions. Most importantly, warriors do not wallow in weakness and self-pity. All true warriors always respect themselves and others, regardless of how much weight they can lift in any gym or competition.

12

General Information for Success

Focus on Form and Technique

The psychological aspects of achieving your ultimate 1RM are almost as important as the physical training leading up to it. Therefore, it is paramount in your last volume single session to create the same psychological approach that you plan to use in the competition. Remember, you are building a recipe for success that is going to be exactly repeatable in the championship.

- Throughout the 1RM Method, I always recommend to avoid training to failure. Never lift to the point that you are grinding out more than your very last rep in any set. Remember, excellent form in training is essential for success in powerlifting and most especially for achieving the best possible 1RM.
- The big problem with less-than-perfect technique is that your body becomes accustomed to lifting this way, which ultimately leads to failed lifts in competitions, plateaus and injuries.
- In many cases, improper form and grinding out lifts increases neural fatigue to such a level that your body cannot recover fully before your next workout.
- This is not to say a bit of a grind on your last rep should never happen. Of course it will! But you are certainly not going to ignore it. Do not continue to perform even more reps, or even worse, increase the weight at the expense of bad technique.
- In my 20 years of powerlifting, I notice that the biggest gains in strength come from reps executed with perfect form. These perfect reps really should challenge the technique without completely breaking it down to an awful grind. Believe me! Performing good technique is where you will always get the biggest increases in strength and training in this manner consistently produces incredible long-term results.

I often hear people arguing the case that perfect form is not critically important, especially when it comes to the rounding of the back involved with the deadlift. My response is simple. If you train with a rounded back, then your potential to lift a true 1RM load is obviously limited because of basic muscle physiology.

The proprioceptors in and around the spine will be sending warning signals to the brain, which in turn will send inhibitory signals back to prime movers (hamstrings, glutes, and back musculature) that will essentially shutdown the muscle contraction needed for achieving a new 1RM. I will not even mention the high price that your nervous system pays! It might take up to two weeks to recover fully from a massive grind on a deadlift.

As a coach, I always tell all of my lifters that the only place it is acceptable to really grind out a lift badly is during a competition. But at the end of the day, if grinding out gets us the win, then go for it! All of that hard work has really paid off! You just got a new Personal Best, and now you are the Champ!

- If you are a competitive powerlifter, then each lift requires very specific lifting criteria and technical form. Otherwise, the referees may not allow the lift. It is very simple. If you lift with bad form, then you are also far less likely to even be allowed the lift on competition day. But if you perform the lifts with near-perfect technique, then you will inevitably get three white lights, get 9 out of 9 lifts, and win the medal!

When following the 1RM Method, or any peaking phase for that matter, always try to maximise your sleep by scheduling it into your diary just like your training sessions. Shoot for 9-hours of *quality sleep* per night, or at least an extra hour compared to your normal sleep schedule post max effort lifting. Nine hours sleep post max effort will help your body better recover.

13

Planning Training Frequency, Peaking and Tapering

Below are examples of how best to organise your training frequency and mesocycle in the build-up to a championship. You should try and work out from previous experience, which mesocycle suits you best. I have offered some very broad generalisations if you are a complete beginner or simply are not sure. The reason I cannot tell you the exact mesocycle is because there are just way too many variables to consider: Age/training age/nutrition/sleep/specific stress/non-specific stress. A number of these variables may also be constantly changing due to any number of reasons.

After nearly two decades of coaching, I have found, time and time again, that in most sports, anything over eight weeks of tapering and prepping for a competition is just too long to achieve any worthwhile results. Athletes tend to become disinterested, start to peak too soon and ultimately become neurologically flat! Likewise, those athletes who try to peak in only two, or even three weeks, generally greatly oversimplify the process and fail to effectively taper or fine tune their nervous system to be able to handle a true 1RM optimal load. This is why it is important to factor in the percentage of loads you are currently using before beginning the 4 week 1RM or the 6 week 1RM Method.

In my experience, the best possible way to peak for a championship is to undulate the volume between high and low weeks, periodically tapering the overall volume throughout this final mesocycle while linearly increasing the loads. Fatigue affects fitness levels, so the 1RM Method reduces the overall volume throughout the program, allowing a gradual tapering effect so that your body's preparedness improves and therefore, allows the super-compensatory effect to occur when it counts the most.

Your body will best adapt to the high-intensity stimuli on low-volume predictor lift weeks and of course, on the final taper days leading up to the championship. You take out dynamic effort method sessions in the final week before the championship, so you will experience very little cumulative fatigue while simultaneously achieving an elevated level of preparedness for the championship.

The 1RM Method is simply creating a high-intensity, linear step loading progression throughout your build-up, with an undulating reduction in volume. This is because research indicates that the volume, not the intensity, is the primary contributor to fatigue. The high-intensity stimuli tend to cause primarily neural adaptations, which tend to occur fairly quickly. The higher volume weeks on the other hand, will have cumulative effects that may take nearly a week from which to recover fully. This cumulative stress, along with the other dynamic effort method sessions will cause a small overreaching effect. This is why you want those crucial full days of recovery before the championship so that your body is fully able to super-compensate before the competition.

By allowing recovery to occur through periodic reductions in volume, you can achieve further increases in intensity during the build-up to your new 1RM. Your body will peak at the precise and appropriate date because of the overall reduction in volume throughout the entire 1RM Method.

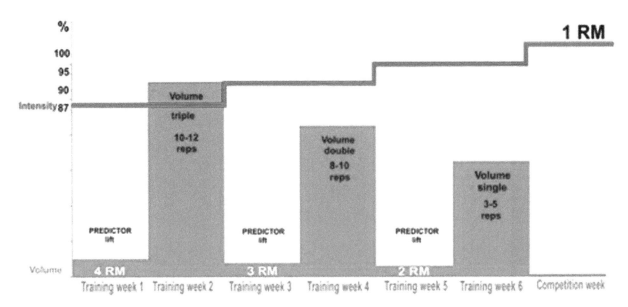

Volume & intensity model

Examples of Final Recovery Days Before a Competition

For the final recovery/taper days, I usually recommend 5–6 days completely off from the squat and deadlift before the competition. In other words, make sure that you get at least 6 days of full recovery after your last squat and last deadlift sessions. Regarding your last bench session, you only generally need 4–5 days of full recovery. This is due to a couple of reasons.

Firstly, you perform only one max effort movement in the session and secondly, the bench press uses smaller muscle groups than the squat and the deadlift with loads that are normally considerably smaller. Therefore, you are not challenging your nervous system as much with the bench as you are with the squat and deadlift. As a result, you should achieve an increase in preparedness and super-compensation much sooner. Obviously, there are exceptions but in my twenty 20 years in the iron game, I have only seen such an exception maybe once or twice in my entire career.

Remember this taper is the norm, so if you are a novice lifting one and a half times your body weight or less, it may be wise to have less of a complete taper as you will accommodate and super-compensate sooner. Likewise, the reverse is true, if you are lifting three or more times your body weight, you will benefit from a slightly longer taper before competing.

13.1 Planning Recovery/Taper

Now, let's get back to some recommended examples of how those final recovery days should look to a powerlifter heading towards victory at the coming championship.

Final taper recovery days for most lifters above 66–83kg or any intermediate lifter handling loads 1½ to 2½ times their body weight, regardless of gender.

I normally recommend four days of full recovery for bench and five days of full recovery for the squat and deadlift. Between four and five days of recovery is necessary to allow the nervous system the adequate time to peak optimally before the championship. Lifting these loads require this sort of time for the lifter to recover fully and super-compensate.

MON	TUE	WED	THU	FRI	SAT	SUN
1x3 Max Triple Squat. 1x3 max triple Deadlift assistant & accessory	Dynamic Bench 2 Assistant & accessory work	4	Dynamic Squat & Deadlift 5 Assistant & accessory work	1x3 Max Triple Bench 6 Assistant & accessory	7	8
5x2 Volume doubles Squat. 4x3 Deadlift triples 80%. Assistant & accessory	Dynamic Bench 10 Assistant & accessory work	11	Dynamic Squat & Deadlift 12 Assistant & accessory work	5x2 Volume doubles 13 Bench. Assistant & accessory	14	(15)
1x2 Max double Squat & Deadlift 16 Assistant & accessory work	Dynamic Bench 17 Assistant & accessory work	18	Dynamic Squat & Deadlift 19 Assistant & accessory work	1x2 Max double Bench 20 Assistant & accessory work	21	22
5x1 Volume doubles Squat. 5x2 Deadlift doubles 85%. Assistant & accessory	5x1 Volume Bench 24 Assistant & accessory	25	26	27	28 Meet	29

MON	TUE	WED	THU	FRI	SAT	SUN
1x4 Max Four squat & Deadlift 1 Assistant & accessory work	Dynamic Bench 2 Assistant & accessory work	3	Dynamic Squat 4 Assistant & accessory work	1x4 Max Four bench 5 Assistant & accessory work	6	7
4x3 Volume triple squat. 4x3 deadlift 80% Assistant & accessory	Dynamic Bench 9 Assistant & accessory work	10	Dynamic Squat 11 Assistant & accessory work	4x3 Volume triple bench 12 Assistant & accessory work	13	14
1x3 Max triple squat & Deadlift 15 Assistant & accessory work	Dynamic Bench 16 Assistant & accessory work	17	Dynamic Squat 18 Assistant & accessory work	1x3 Max triple bench 19 Assistant & accessory work	20	21
5x2 Volume double squat. 5x3 Deadlift triples 80% Assistant &	Dynamic Bench 23 Assistant & accessory	24	Dynamic Squat 25 Assistant & accessory	5x2 Volume double bench. 26 Assistant & accessory	27	28
1x2 Max Double squat & Deadlift 1 Assistant & accessory work	Dynamic Bench 1 Assistant & accessory work	2	Dynamic Squat 3 Assistant & accessory work	1x2 Max double bench. 4 Assistant & accessory work	5	6
5x1 Volume single squat. 5x2 Deadlift doubles 85%. Assistant & accessory	5x1 Volume single bench 8 Assistant & accessory work	9	10	11	12	13 Meet

Final taper recovery days for most lifters above 93–120kg or any advanced lifter handling loads 2–3 times their body weight, regardless of gender.

It is always important to take into consideration the lifter's body weight when considering the rest times and appropriate tapering strategy. Larger lifters simply have much more muscle fibre that needs to recover fully when compared to smaller lifters. They also tend to perform using heavier max loads. In these cases, I typically recommend five days of full recovery for bench and six days of full recovery for the squat and deadlift. Again, this extra day of recovery is necessary to allow the nervous system the adequate time to peak optimally before the championship, because the related larger loads lifted requires more time for the lifter to recover fully and super-compensate.

Mon	Tue	Wed	Thu	Fri	Sat	Sun
	1	2	3	4	5	1x3 Max Triple Squat, 1x3 max triple Deadlift assistant & accessory
7	1x3 Max triple Bench, Assistant & accessory work	Dynamic Squat & deadlift, Assistant & accessory work	10	11	Dynamic Bench, Assistant & accessory work	5x2 Volume doubles Squat 4x3 Deadlift triples BO', Assistant & accessory
14	5x2 Volume doubles Bench Assistant & accessory	Dynamic Squat & deadlift, Assistant & accessory work	17	18	Dynamic Bench, Assistant & accessory work	1x2 Max double Squat 1x2 max double Deadlift assistant & accessory
21	1x2 Max double Bench Assistant & accessory work	23	24	25	5x1 Volume doubles Squat 5x2 Deadlift doubles BO', Assistant & accessory	5x1 Volume Bench Assistant & accessory
28	29	30	31		Meet	

Final taper recovery days for the biggest, strongest lifters or any advanced lifter handling loads 3–4 times their body weight, regardless of gender.

I normally recommend six days of full recovery for the bench and seven days of full recovery for the squat and deadlift for the strongest lifters. Lifting incredible loads like these requires a considerable length of time for the central nervous system to recover fully, peak, and generate the desired super-compensation effect required to win the gold!

Final taper recovery days for very high-frequency lifters, regardless of gender.

When coaching lifters who have spent several months or even years squatting and benching nearly every other day, I have found that, occasionally, the lift mechanics can suffer as a result of not regularly lifting. Movement patterns seemingly break down unless they maintain a reasonably high frequency of at least every 72–48 hours.

For these types of lifters, I find that they can benefit greatly by performing a light mini-meet about 72–48-hours before the competition. In this mini-meet, the lifter only performs the dynamic effort method for 2–3 sets at 55–60% of their 1RM. If this is you, then always make sure to walk away thinking that you could have successfully lifted even more, because your primary objective is to avoid all possibility of fatigue. All you have to do is simply keep the movement pattern fresh. This lighter mini-meet can also provide the lifters with numerous psychological benefits by providing additional practice with executing the lifts under command.

13.2 Setting up your Planned Microcycle / Training Frequency

I have listed the three most common options for setting up your training schedule.

You can set up your training frequency any number of ways with the 1RM Method. Here are some of my favourite ways, along with some reasons why I like them:

MON	TUE	WED	THU	FRI	SAT	SUN
14	15	16	17	1x4 Max four Squat & Deadlift. Assistant & accessory	19	20
Dynamic Squat & Deadlift. Assistant & accessory	1x4 Max four Bench. Assistant & accessory	23	Dynamic Bench. Assistant & accessory	4x3 Volume triple Squat, 4x3 Deadlift triples 80% Assisant & accessory	26	27
Dynamic Squat & Deadlift Assistant & accessory	4x3 Volume triple Bench. Assistant & accessory work	30	Dynamic Bench. Assistant & accessory	1x3 Max triple Squat & Deadlift. Assistant & accessory		
Dynamic Squat & Bench. Deadlift. Assistant & accessory	1x3 Max triple Bench. Assistant & accessory	6	Dynamic Bench. Assistant & accessory	5x2 Volume double Squat, 4x3 Deadlift triples 80% Assistant & accessory	9	10
Dynamic Squat & Deadlift. Assistant & accessory	5x2 Volume double Bench. Assistant & accessory work	13	Dynamic Bench. Assistant & accessory	1x2 Max double Squat & Deadlift. Assistant & accessory	16	17
Dynamic Squat & Deadlift. Assistant & accessory	1x2 Max double Bench. Assistant & accessory	20	21	5x1 Volume single Squat, 85% 4x2 deadlifts	5x1 Volume single Bench. Assistant & accessory	24
25	26 Mini meet	27	28	29	30 meet	31

Option #1

Day 1 (Monday):	Max effort, squat and deadlift
Day 2 (Tuesday):	Dynamic effort, bench
Day 3 (Wednesday):	Off
Day 4 (Thursday):	Dynamic effort, squat and deadlift
Day 5 (Friday):	Max effort, bench
Day 6 (Saturday):	Off
Day 7 (Sunday):	Off

Option #2

Day 1 (Monday):	Off
Day 2 (Tuesday):	Max effort, squat and deadlift
Day3 (Wednesday):	Dynamic effort, bench
Day 4 (Thursday):	Off
Day 5 (Friday):	Dynamic effort, squat and deadlift
Day 6 (Saturday):	Max effort, bench
Day 7 (Sunday):	Off

Option #3

Day 1 (Monday):	Max effort, squat and deadlift
Day 2 (Tuesday):	Dynamic effort, bench
Day3 (Wednesday):	Off
Day 4 (Thursday):	Off
Day 5 (Friday):	Dynamic effort, squat and deadlift
Day 6 (Saturday):	Max effort, bench
Day 7 (Sunday):	Off

As you can see, I prefer to split up the max effort sessions. By separating them, I find that you generally witness much better results regarding increased motivation and reduced levels of tiredness. Through the use of feedback/training logs and using the Bio-Force HRV system with some of my more elite level lifters these findings have been further validated. The HRV system allows me to quantify the cumulative stress levels from training better than any other system/method I have used. This system puts daily RPE and other similar methods to shame.

Now, I do not want to rave on and on about HRV, but I can say this, it has a definite influence on my overall professional training strategies as well as on the 1RM Method. By implementing HRV into your 1RM Method, what you will see, time and time again, is that organising your training schedule as much as possible into "hard days" followed by "easy days" helps you to promote recovery and adaptation. Research shows, consistently, that the body always responds more positively to what are called *high-low days*, even in strength-related sports like powerlifting.

When creating your training frequencies, keep in mind that most competitions occur on the weekends (Saturday or Sunday). By following one of my recommended schedules, you can essentially drop the dynamic effort days from the last week as a way to create a taper in overall volume. Then, simply move the max effort sessions together, which gives you between 4–7 days to recover fully and to optimise your 1RM for the upcoming competition.

As you can see from the program outline above, I am a firm believer in placing squats and deadlifts together because, like I have said before, that's exactly what happens at a meet. In this regard, the program is sport-specific. At a championship, you might only have a break of around 40 minutes to, perhaps, a few hours' break between the squat event and the deadlift event. Training both of these lifts together will only benefit you at the all-important championship.

Bearing this in mind, your gym training deadlift maximum weight will not usually be as great as your competition maximum, due to the increased recovery time between movements in most competitions. Therefore, be prepared that you might actually be capable of achieving a greater weight in the meet than previously expected, based on your max triple or doubles coming into the meet.

14

Attempt Selection

This may sound strange, but it is 100% true! It is quite rare to see lifters hitting their true 1RM at competitions and this is because they seem to rather pre-fatigue themselves during their warm-ups, or perhaps, they may simply have an extremely poor attempt selection. A poor attempt selection can also cause fatigue between attempts or simply does not allow the nervous system to get fired up effectively enough to handle the next attempt, which ultimately leads to a decreased 1RM.

There are some other systems for peaking that are simply way too subjective to be beneficial in the build-up phase to an important championship. These other systems may be focusing strictly on daily RPE's, which simply will not give you accurate feedback during the peaking phase to make the correct decisions regarding attempt selections. Take it from me, in 2015, I coached the team with the best attempt selection in the world. You should be able to recognise my lifters in any competition; they are the ones going 7 for 9 on a bad day; 9 for 9 is what we expected and that's why we win.

By performing the 1RM Method, you will have all the feedback that you need to make the best possible decision on the day of the competition. The only thing you need to do is respect the fact that your 1RM is a dynamic variable that can change from day to day. So listen to your body instead of relying on some random 1RM calculator or some rubbish RPE you performed a week ago. The body's natural form of feedback is always the best calculator to achieve a new Personal Best on the day of the competition.

14.1 Competition Day Attempt Selections

If you are a novice lifter, I would normally recommend that you open with a slighter lighter load than that of your max triple, then simply base your second attempt on how that max triple feels and on the weight used in your max double attempt during the build-up to the championship. In doing so, you get two very important points of reference. The first, and probably the most important point, is that it helps you predict how the lift felt and how well your body has responded to the taper. The second point is that it helps determine your true lifting capabilities on the day, accounting for any stress the competition has created. In some ways, the second attempt is the most crucial because this attempt should give you all the accurate, up-to-the-minute, feedback that influences the third and final attempt selection.

If you are a stronger, more advanced lifter, then you might be comfortable opening a little heavier than your max triple instead of lighter. As a general rule, your incremental increases in loads between lifts will be slightly higher than those of novice or intermediate lifters but the principles above are still valid.

Remember, it is all about your second attempt. The second attempt influences your choice of weight for the crucial third and final attempt. If selected wisely, the second attempt will help build a bigger overall total while simultaneously priming the nervous system and giving you all the feedback you need to select your third and final attempt *without incurring too much fatigue.*

Remember, always try to plan ahead to make sure that the loads are decreasing slightly between each attempt. This allows for better potentiation of the nervous system while building up to a 1RM.

Your first attempt should be your last warm-up set. There should be no doubt in your mind that you will successfully get the lift.

On the day of the competition, your opener is the best time to finalise your mental preparation for the actual event. This is when you can adjust your thinking to cognitively process commands in the new and unfamiliar environment, while working with a warm-up weight. After all, you do not want to make an official attempt that requires every bit of your mental focus if you are not 100% mentally prepared, simply because of your surroundings.

The first attempt should prime your nervous system for the second attempt. The second attempt should further prime your nervous system for your estimated third and final attempt. As a result, the second attempt is an extremely important lift for a number of reasons:

- The second attempt selection will build a reasonable total.
- Most importantly, the second attempt gives you the essential feedback for the most important attempt selection of the day, the third and final attempt.
- In general, the incremental weight decreases between each successful attempt.

If you are new to competitive powerlifting, then I suggest opening light. Select a weight that you can easily triple, even on a bad day. Never open too heavy. You do not want to risk *bombing out* and you definitely do not want to be fighting an uphill battle both mentally and physically. Opening too heavy will generally be an indication that you have structured your warm-up incorrectly, which will inevitably lead to unnecessary increased fatigue. All of this extra stress will wreak havoc on your confidence, leaving you far less likely to achieve your intended 1RM.

So, always select an opening weight that you can comfortably lift and look good lifting at the same time. The judges will take notice and likely begin to view you in a very positive light as a worthy competitor. Otherwise, they might become overly critical for when it counts the most your third and final attempt.

The second attempt is not the time to take risks either. As a general rule, never go for your Personal Best during the second attempt. The second attempt is more about building a big total. Even though you will incorporate larger weight increases between your first and second attempt, you should still play it smart.

I cannot stress this enough! The second attempt is more about building a good total and getting a feel for what you estimate your true 1RM to be on competition day.

For the third and final attempt, target a weight that is between 97% and 103% of your estimated 1RM. *Yes, I did say 103%!* I personally like to use three options on all of my lifters' final attempts and prepare to go anywhere in between them if needed.

- **The first option** on the third attempt is playing it safe, taking an easy third attempt to secure an individual medal and/or help build an overall total without risking anything.
- **The second option** on all of the final attempts will usually be at a 100% 1RM if everything is progressing according to plan.
- **The third option** could be as much as 103% of your estimated 1RM, maybe more on the deadlift. In some cases, I only use this option if everything is going extremely well or if there is a medal at stake. However, you have to be certain that you can make it and weigh everything up properly! You do not want to see your chances of medalling go down the drain by missing a lift.

The only time that you do not have to try so hard to weigh everything up properly by calculating your sub-total and taking your competitor's sub-total into account is when executing the deadlift. If reaching for 103% or more of your 1RM means potentially winning a medal and not risking anything, then just go for it!

Of course, there is far more strategy involved with international elite-level powerlifting. After all, lifters can win medals for each different lift. So, if you are not competing at this elite-level, then in most cases you should probably avoid going beyond your estimated 100% 1RM on the squat and bench, as it is generally not worth risking your total.

14.2 Smart Attempt Selection Example:

Squat

- 1st attempt: 200kg This was the successful max triple predictor lift
- 2nd attempt: 215kg This was the successful max double predictor lift estimated 95%
- 3rd attempt: A safe 225kg, which was just below the estimated 100% 1RM based on max triple and double predictor lifts

Bench

- 1st attempt: 140kg This was the successful max triple predictor lift
- 2nd attempt: 150kg This was the successful max double predictor lift estimated 95%
- 3rd attempt: A safe 155kg which was just below the estimated 98% 1RM based on max triple and double predictor lifts

Deadlift

- 1st attempt: 230kg This was the successful max triple predictor lift
- 2nd attempt: 245kg This was the successful max double predictor lift estimated 95%
- 3rd attempt: 257.5kg which was about the estimated 100% based on max triple and double lifts

(Using the warm-up and attempt selection template provided below will eliminate most of the guesswork on the day of the competition, allowing you to focus on competing and having the best possible outcome rather than worrying about what weights you will be lifting).

Attempt selection sheets

1st 2nd 3rd attempt & Warm up Form

Name

Weight class

	Squat			Bench			Deadlift		
Competition PB									
Estimated 1rm									
Max triple									
Max double									

	Squat			Bench			Deadlift		
Hard third atten									
Estimated 1RM									
Safe third attem									
Secound Attemp									
First Attempt									
Warm Up									

	Squat			Bench			Deadlift		
	rest	Weight	Rep	rest	Weight	Rep	rest	Weight	Rep

Above is the same attempt selection template I created for Great Britain Powerlifting Team.

14.3 Detailed Attempt Selections Information

Each attempt primes the nervous system for the following attempt. Therefore, it is critical to get your attempt selection criteria correct if you are aiming to achieve your ultimate 1RM, especially during a competition, when it truly counts.

By performing the 1RM Method, you get the most accurate feedback needed to make the best possible attempt selection on the day of the competition. As the saying goes, *"Failing to plan is planning to fail"*.

First Attempt

The first attempt is very important for a variety of reasons. If you were to miss this critical first attempt, then you could write off any chance of getting a new Personal Best on the lift in question. It is also highly unlikely that you will get a Personal Best Total at the end of the day, assuming that you do not completely bomb out of the competition altogether.

If you happen to miss that first attempt, then I would never recommend increasing the weight on the second attempt; not unless the miss is due to some sort of technical error like a slight movement of the foot during the lift. In this case, you might consider increasing the weight, but definitely not to the level you were originally planning. After all, you do not want to take any chances of bombing out!

Remember, there is always a chance that you might simply be having a bad day. Maximum strength is a dynamic variable. It changes from day to day and there is always a risk that you could miss your pre-planned second attempt. So, it is usually wise to keep the second attempt at the same weight as the first, in most cases. Only then will you be able to re-evaluate for the third attempt successfully. Otherwise, the incremental increases between lifts might be too great for your nervous system to handle effectively.

A not-so-well-considered fact, but a very important reason behind opening with a comfortable first attempt, is that referees are only human. Take advantage of this fact. What I mean by this is that by showing the referee excellent technique on your first attempt, they will almost always be far less critical of you on the second and third attempts. The referees will usually give you the benefit if there is any doubt and award you the lift.

I always tell my powerlifters that the first attempt is the last warm-up. So give the referee what they want! Lift around an estimated 90–94% of your 1RM so that you are always very confident that you will never miss this lift, even on your worst day. By performing your last warm-up under command, while in the same unfamiliar space as the competition, using the same equipment and in full view of strangers and referees, your chances of hitting those critical second and third attempts and winning the competition are already significantly improved.

It is very simple to plan your attempt selections with the 1RM Method. Your max triple should be roughly your first attempt of the day and this will generally be at 90–94% of your 1RM.

Second Attempt

The second attempt will usually be roughly the same lifting weight as the max double that you perform in the build-up phase. It will give you all the accurate feedback needed to assess the effectiveness of the previous tapering and peaking phases, allowing you to make the best possible choice for your third and final attempt.

The second attempt should not be a grinder because you do not want to create unwanted energy leaks and flatten out your nervous system. In general, shoot for around 94–97% of your 1RM so that you will likely fall within 6–3% of your estimated 1RM on all of your second attempts. The goal is to achieve a good total and still prime your nervous system to get ready for that crucial 1RM.

97% may sound rather high, but remember, if you are utilizing the 1RM Method properly, then no cumulative fatigue from previous workouts will affect your 1RM potential because you have successfully reduced the volume in the last microcycle. In reality, most powerlifters using this system are easily capable of plus 100–103% of the estimated 1RM calculated from their max triple or double. This is because there will always be some cumulative fatigue from previous workouts when performing these max effort predictor lifts. So the improvement and potential to lift above your estimated 100% exists once you factor in the reduced volume in the final microcycle, which allows increased preparedness and the super-compensation effect to take place.

Third and Final Attempt

This third and final attempt is the big one, the attempt that you have been working so hard to maximise. After performing that crucial second attempt, you should be able to visualise how the weight will feel and what exactly you are capable of lifting on this third attempt. However, there is no shame in playing it safe or in equalling a previous Personal Best or less if this means giving you a better chance of achieving a bigger overall total as a result.

I cannot count the total number of medals we have won internationally by playing it safe when everyone else is trying to out-lift each other. All too often, the competition misses, essentially handing us the medal when we easily get the lift. So remember, before selecting your third and final attempt, always be realistic and allow your second attempt to guide your final decision. Then simply give it your best shot to factor in what you assume your overall total will be, compared to the other lifters that you are battling. Then it is time to get the job done and take the competition!

Remember, records are fleeting, someone will always beat them, but no one can take medals and championship victories away from you.

15

Understanding where and how much assistant and accessory exercise to perform.

Because peaking for a Powerlifting meet relies on high-intensity training protocols to get results, there is a fine balance between peaking and overtraining. Rest and regeneration are essential for an increased 1RM and to avoid any injuries that may be caused through the repetitive nature of the sport.

This may sound obvious, but it is very important to understand that the sport of powerlifting requires training sessions consisting of lots of squatting, benching, and deadlifting. Like any sports enthusiast who wants to compete and win in the competitive arena, you have to devote a great deal of time to your sport. So, do not waste too much time on those assistance and accessory exercises during this competition phase.

For example, some powerlifters tend to spend less time squatting, benching, deadlifting during the GPP phase while instead devoting reasonable amounts of training time to more general exercises to try and build a better foundation, which, in my opinion, is a very sensible approach to reduce chances of injury and increase long term progression and ultimately success.

The reduction in overall volume and exposure to sport specific movement will decrease the risks of possible injury while also reducing the chances of plateauing on key sporting movements. Let's say that I am building a race car and only focus on increasing the BHP (brake horsepower) of the engine. I will inevitably run into problems if I were not to equally improve the strength of the chassis to handle the new increased levels of power produced by the engine.

Okay, so let's get back on-point. In the final realisation/peaking phase, which is exactly what the 1RM Method is all about, you should be focussing on the realisation of the full maximal strength potential you have been developing over the last 3, 6 or even 12 months. That is to say, you need to devote most of your time and effort on key lifts and less time on assistance and accessories exercises so that you have the ability to recover fully. You should be aware of the cumulative effects of fatigue from session to session while also understanding that performing too many general exercises will only reduce your strength, potential substantially. Remember, your primary goal during this phase of training is to achieve maximum realisation to boost your 1RM to the highest level possible.

In general, I usually recommend that strong and very strong lifters reduce the number of assistance exercises while performing the 1RM Method. Focus only on performing a very small number of movements that consist of similar motor patterns used with the three big lifts. The reason for this is that lifters who can squat 300kg need a great deal more time for the nervous system to recover fully than a beginner powerlifter who can only squat around 150kg. If you think you will benefit from more volume in your workouts, then add more accessory exercises that target smaller intrinsic muscle groups.

15.1 Choosing Appropriate Assistance Exercises

Assistance work is exactly what the name implies – they provide *assistance* in building strength in the key lifts that you need to improve. To put this another way, assistance exercises will generally have the same or similar motor pattern as the related key lift, helping you to improve the weak points to successfully achieve needed strength throughout the full range of movement.

If you choose correctly, assistant exercises can improve overall posture and symmetry, while increasing muscle mass and strength in the proper areas to again, assist in lifting larger weights on the three main lifts.

For these reasons, I generally only perform a maximum of about eight reps of 40 seconds or less time under tension (TUT) on these movements. By training within 20–40 seconds TUT, you will gain what is called *functional hypertrophy*. Functional hypertrophy is simply the process of gaining muscle mass that recruits high threshold motor units, the ones that are used in maximal effort lifting.

- As a general rule of thumb, unless you are in a general preparation phase (GPP), do not spend too much time and effort focusing on assistance or accessory exercises. It is very important to remember that there is always a cost to everything you do. By spending more time and energy performing lots of assistance or accessory exercises in a specific preparation phase (SPP) or competition phase, you end up with far less training time and energy for improving the specific movements needed to boost your 1RM. You may be better off simply focussing on recovering fully and preparing yourself to get ready to *smash out* the next big lifting session to prepare for the competition.
- My advice is to do a maximum of 1–2 assistance exercises for the lower body to target those muscle groups used for squatting and deadlifting.
- I suggest performing 2–3 assistance exercise for the upper body. These smaller muscle groups are only capable of lifting less weight. Therefore, you will recover faster, from a neuromuscular standpoint, which means that you can afford to do a little more overall volume of exercise and still recovery optimally.
- Another tip, maybe just one of my own personal pet peeves, is do not waste any time or energy on abs, calves, or forearms during the competition phase. These types of exercises offer very little direct carryover to the key lifts at this point in your training.
- Bigger and stronger lifters will generally benefit from performing smaller accessory exercises as these will not overly impact nervous system recovery between sessions.
- Bigger and stronger lifters will also need to do less heavy assistance exercise to better allow the nervous system to recover between sessions.
- Smaller novice lifters will generally benefit from performing slightly more heavy assistance exercise as these will not overly impact nervous system recovery.

So remember, the selection of assistance and accessory exercises performed during this phase are essential to your success in the coming competition. The proper combination is important to offset any faulty intrinsic mechanics that might have a negative effect on you reaching your optimum 1RM. Therefore, do not waste your time and energy on abs, calves, or forearm exercises during the peaking phase.

What is the difference between Accessory and Assistance Exercises?

Accessory exercises can be defined as any exercise the does not have a similar motor pattern to the lifts that you perform in a competition. I like to use accessory exercises to improve faulty intrinsic mechanics while also helping to prevent possible injury and improve asymmetrical imbalances simultaneously.

Some accessory exercises target similar small intrinsic muscle groups used in key movements, so you should never begin your workout with accessory exercises that focus on these important muscle groups. After all, you do not want these muscles to be overly fatigued right before you need them to stabilize key lifts. That can be extremely dangerous. You will likely produce a negative effect on your overall lifting stability, essentially reducing the ability to perform true max effort lifts.

- To get the optimum benefits from your selected accessory exercises, performing them with higher reps 9–12 at around 50–60 sec TUT usually works best as a general rule.
- Never superset the key lift you are trying to develop in a competition phase, but your B, C and D exercises will always benefit from super setting as much as possible. Supersets help increase the density of the workout, reduce overall training time and therefore, maximise your ability to recover fully between workouts.

15.2 Designing your Program: Suggestions on Assistance and Accessory Exercises

Let's recall one very important fact. During any peaking, realisation, or transmutation phase (whatever you want to call it), *less is more*. That being said, if you are a novice or a smaller intermediate athlete who does not lift as great a weight, in most cases your neuromuscular system will get adequate recovery between workouts without much pre-planning on your part. For this reason, you might benefit from working in a relatively large level of assistance and accessory exercises in this peaking phase. You could even choose to perform more than two assistance exercises per workout that focus on developing targeted strength improvements in the weaker point of your lifts. Or you could choose to do exercises that include lifting supramaximal weights, allowing the neuromuscular system to better accommodate heavier loads, in order to better prepare you for a 1RM. This is something I do with all my lifters in an SPP Phase of training.

A good example would be performing rack pulls in cases where you want to improve a weak lockout. It is important to remember however, that the potential to increase a great deal of strength within the weak portion of any lift is limited during any peaking phase of training. Do not waste too much time and energy on assistance exercises. They will only provide a rather small improvement, at best. In the case of a very strong lifter, too much heavy assistant work could negatively affect your recovery between sessions. In other words, if the volume of high intensity work is too great, your nervous system will not adapt positively.

Remember, when you are performing assistance exercises that directly resemble the motor patterns used within competitive lifts (squats, benching, deadlifting), you will need to adjust your workout accordingly as your load weights continue to increase. After all, you do not want to incur neuromuscular fatigue. For very strong lifters, reducing the amount of assistance exercise will allow your nervous system to really peak for that pending championship battle.

How much is too much volume when it comes to assistance and accessory exercises?
That is the million-dollar question! In my experience, most of the more successful coaches can nail down this number after only one trial run at the weekly training frequency, providing all things being the same.

Let me explain. What I mean when I say *"all things being the same"* is that it is always essential to factor in both the specific stress and the non-specific stress of the lifter, as I previously stated. Do not forget to take into consideration those stresses that result from everyday life such as quality of sleep, quality of nutrition, family life and work life. All of these have an effect on your body's ability to recover fully.

A good coach will always try to get his or her athletes to keep a training log. The athlete then writes down all related training data including:

- **How well the athlete is sleeping on a daily basis.**
- **The daily diet of the athlete.**
- **Unforeseen additional daily stress factors, both specific and non-specific.**
- **All lifts and exercises performed within each session.**
- **And most importantly, how tough each session is to complete, or the RPE.**

If the athlete's overall daily rating is very high, the coach might drop some volume performed on assistance and accessory exercises. If the previous daily rating was very high and the athlete clearly will not be able to perform at the necessary level to achieve a positive effect, then it might be wise for the coach to instruct the athlete to take a day off by dropping the training session altogether.

An example of this scenario might be when a lifter has an incredibly stressful day at work before heading to the gym to attempt a max effort predictor lift session. The athlete logs a high daily RPE score, then to make things even worse, gets a terrible night's sleep due to all of this excess work-related stress. The next day, the lifter shows up for a dynamic effort session feeling extremely tired. If the coach is smart, then he or she might suggest skipping this dynamic session all together while opting to refocus on recovering fully to better maximise the previous predictor lift session and be properly ready for the next planned session.

As a very general rule, I recommend that novice lifters are able to adequately perform up to 2 assistance exercises with large loads at 90–110% of their 1RM for up to four sets each exercise in a peaking phase.
For intermediate athletes, I recommend only performing one or two assistance exercises at 90–110% of their 1RM for up to four sets in a peaking phase.

For more advance lifters, I recommend that they only perform up to one assistance exercise at 90–110% of their 1RM for no more than four sets to allow the best possible positive adaptation between sessions.

Performing up to 110% of your 1RM on an assistance exercise means if your predicted 1RM on bench is 150KG and you are performing a high board press as an assistance exercise post bench press, the weight could possibly be as high as 165KG for doubles. However, if you can handle a greater load, it is best to be slightly conservative to allow for adequate nervous system recovery to allow peaking can occur.

15.3 Planning Assistance and Accessory Exercises

- *Individual Limiting Factors:* The right way to choose assistance and accessory exercises should be based on your individual limiting factors. A good example of an assistance exercise for someone who struggles to lockout a deadlift might be a rack pull. The small ROM, higher start position, and the similar movements involved, normally allow you to get a tighter back position and lift maximal loads for more reps. You also are more likely to lift supra-maximal loads for the same number of reps, all of which can help improve your ability to lockout in the deadlift and better accustom your neuromuscular system for hitting a new 1RM at the up-coming competition.

Assistance exercises are generally considered to have a similar motor pattern to the exercises they are assisting, so can create more neural fatigue as a result. You should, therefore, factor this into the planning of your overall program.

- *Training Age:* If you are a lifter with a high training age and high levels of maximal strength, then you will want to keep assistance exercises to the bare minimum during the peaking phase to allow full recovery between sessions. I have had many discussions with Tony Cliffie, who is currently the biggest and strongest unequipped raw lifter in Great Britain and he only squats once every seven days! Tony squats well over 330kg (730 lbs) during competition and over 290kg (640 lbs) during training. How many times do you think he, (or any other unenhanced, unequipped, raw lifter for that matter) can realistically move this sort of weight and still recover fully within a training week with multiple squat sessions? NOT MANY, is the answer!

If you do have a high training age and are at the top of your training potential, then you might benefit from executing only one assistance exercise in order to limit neural fatigue, while increasing the chances of realising a full recovery between sessions. It might even be wise to focus on performing more accessory exercises instead of the assistance movement, since these exercises target smaller muscle groups that do not consist of similar motor patterns to key movements.

Balance Capabilities: Very few powerlifters have good structural balance, particularly in the shoulders. This is likely due to the fact that powerlifters tend to perform lots of bench and pressing movements, which recruit the subscapularis to a high degree. The subscapularis is an internal rotator, which will get a great deal of work in nearly all pressing movements and essentially creates an imbalance between the internal and external rotator cuff. If not addressed, this imbalance can easily lead to a protracted shoulder position, which is very common in powerlifters. If you want to get a foot up on the competition, then a good accessory exercise to offset all of this pressing would be an external rotation for the teres minor and infraspinatus. In addition, performing some rows for the scapula retractors is very helpful for avoiding/correcting this imbalance.

- *Strength Levels:* Another factor to consider when selecting assistance and accessory exercises is the individual strength of the lifter. If you are a more advanced lifter and have a very high level of maximal strength, then you will undoubtedly need more time for your nervous system to recover. As a result, you probably will not want to do as many assistance or even accessory exercises as a novice or intermediate lifter with a lower level of maximal strength. This is one of the major reasons why novice lifters tend to benefit greatly from higher volume training systems, initially. The novice's greater ability to recover fully and at a much faster rate is also why we see so many newbies get such great results so quickly in the early stages of their lifting careers.
- *Size of the Lifter:* You should always be factoring in the size (or body weight) of the lifter when choosing appropriate rest, accessory, and assistance exercises. In general, bigger individuals take longer to recover in between exercise and even training sessions compared to their smaller counterparts. So you see, being a novice to powerlifting *definitely* has its advantages!

Do not forget, in the final taper week it is doubtful that you will have any meaningful increase in strength through performing assistant exercises with a similar motor patterns to your key lifts. Therefore, I generally recommend only focussing on smaller accessory exercises, if needed.

Unfortunately, I cannot simply write the exact assistance and accessory exercise program without performing biomechanical screenings and or other tests to pinpoint limiting factors. This is where a good coach will be looking to reduce the chances of injury and improve the chances of long-term, sustainable improvements.

Without at least a one-on-one consultation, I would find it nearly impossible to tell you how many and which assistance or accessory exercises to perform because no two lifters are exactly alike. We each live very different lives with different stress factors and widely divergent combinations of genetics. Once you begin to also take into consideration the different sleeping and eating habits between lifters, you can quickly begin to see that creating your own accessory and assistance exercise program must be specifically designed for the individual lifter.

But even with all of these constantly changing and uniquely different variables, I would still stick to the old adage, "Less is more".
Remember the ultimate goal of the 1RM Method is to increase your single repetition maximum strength, at a specific moment in the future, like for a competition, for example. Determining and overcoming your individual limiting factors during the general preparation phases of your training regimen is very important to your overall success in future competition.

16

MAKING WEIGHT ON COMPETITION DAY

93kg Jason Coultman 2016 IPF World championships Texas

WATER LOADING for 2 HOUR WEIGH INS

First Things First...

Everything I am about to briefly outline is mainly from personal experience of what I have done leading up to competitions and what I have found works best for me. I am not saying it is the best or only way, because I am well aware that there are many alternative methods. Rather, I am sharing this with you to give you a relatively sound starting point, or simply, just another option to what you might have previously read or heard about.

WHY CUT WEIGHT IN THE FIRST PLACE?

For optimal performance, the aim should be to enter that competition at the very top of your respective weight class, carrying as much muscle as possible whilst still making weight. The most important aspect of cutting weight relatively quickly without the loss of strength is the smart manipulation of water to drop water weight from the body.

CONSIDERATIONS BEFORE DECIDING TO CUT WATER WEIGHT

The first thing you need determine before manipulating water intake is whether or not cutting weight is even necessary. There are two main things to consider in order to determine this:

1) **At what stage are you in your lifting career?**
If you are a novice lifter competing for the first time, or in competitions that are not of massive importance or significance, then rapid weight cuts, whatever the technique, are pointless and absolutely unnecessary. If you do not have a serious shot at winning your weight class, qualifying for a more important/significant competition or breaking a record, then cutting weight should not be a priority. Rather, focus on training to improve technical proficiency, get stronger and enjoy gaining competition experience and hitting some PB's!

2) **What is your body composition?**
As previously stated, the aim is to maximise muscle mass whilst still making weight. This means that you need to be relatively lean in order to maximise your competitiveness on competition day. As a general guideline, I suggest ensuring that your body fat (BF) does not go above 15% for males and above 22% for females. Firstly, because if your BF is much higher than these levels, you are effectively wasting precious weight in the form of fat. A competitor that weighs the same as you but has a lower BF percentage and therefore, more lean body mass (LBM) will be at a competitive advantage. Secondly, if you plan to compete at a lower weight to that which you currently are, being much over these BF values will leave you with a lot of work to do when it comes to getting leaner and dropping the extra weight before a competition.

I suggest that if your BF is higher than these guideline values, then cutting water should not be your first priority to make weight. Rather, your first step should be to alter your body composition to reduce BF and increase LBM. Following a sensible nutrition plan to gradually increase LBM will also likely lead to a reduction in overall body weight and there may well be no need to water cut at all. On the other hand, for a lifter who is relatively lean with a BF percentage closer to 12% or lower, water manipulation may be the best way to allow them to make weight without sacrificing LBM (or muscle).

The aim is, therefore, to train closer to, but not above the threshold BF guidelines given above to allow for sufficient food intake for strength gains and recovery. I will not put a limit on how low BF should be because factors such as age, genetics, muscle mass, and dietary habits will mean that everyone's performance will be effected differently at different BF levels. This means you, as an individual lifter, will have to figure out what is best for you personally, through trial and error, trying different foods and eating habits until you find what is optimal for you.

16.1 WHEN TO CUT WATER WEIGHT

Here are the scenarios/criteria when water manipulation to cut weight will probably be a good option:

- You are an experienced lifter with a serious chance to win or place at your next competition or set a new record.
- You are relatively lean with a BF percentage of around 12% or lower if male and 17% or lower if female.
- Your current weight leaves you sitting just above the borderline of one weight class limit and at the mid to lower end of the next weight class up.

Note: All of these scenarios/criteria should apply to you before deciding to do a weight cut to compete in a lower weight class.

HOW TO CUT WATER

Planning and Preparation

The following protocol is one that I have used, time and time again, to successfully make weight for the 93kg class with a weigh in 2-hours before lifting, both in the UK and abroad after long haul flights. Between competitions, I normally walk around anywhere between 96 and 99kg (dependent on how long I have between each competition) without having to have massive restrictions on my diet and this surplus is advantageous for training and strength gains. I have used the 1RM Method multiple times to great effect and, as Coach Farncombe says, it is all about having a great plan to be at your strongest and win medals. This same approach is the key to a successful water cut and you need to have one eye on the ball a few months in advance.

I advise keeping weight loss for competition through cutting water to a **maximum** of 3kg. You can lose more than this, but with only a 2-hour window, it is unlikely you will be able to sufficiently rehydrate before lifting commences and your performance will likely be compromised. I have cut 3kg of water before multiple competitions and still set PB's in individual lifts and PB totals in competition, despite the cut. So I can confidently say that for me, a 3kg cut has minimal effect on performance.

When aiming to cut 3kg of water, I suggest you should be within 3–4kg of your competition weight **4 weeks** out from the meet and then maintain this weight. The reason for this is because, in line with the 1RM Method, 4 weeks prior to competition day you will be aiming to lift from 90% up to 97% of your 1RM in order to ready your body for a new 1RM and also to get a good indicator of your attempt selections in competition. It therefore makes sense that you perform these lifts at the same or similar weight you plan to be on competition day in order to give you the most accurate feedback. For example, if you are planning to compete in the 93kg class but do all your heavy lifting during the 4-week competition/peaking phase weighing 99kg, then try to lift even heavier than this on competition day when you are 5 or 6kg lighter, it will feel very unfamiliar and you will most likely struggle to lift what you were capable of at your heavier weight. So yes, you will need to start slowly dieting down a few months in advance if you are more than 3–4kg above competition weight. I say 3–4kg because the aim is to loose 3kg of water and then put this weight back on through rehydration immediately after the weigh in. Also, bear in mind that, in addition to losing water weight, you are most likely to also lose a little body weight during the last week of the competition phase due to generally eating a lot more carefully than usual and training less.

The Nitty Gritty – Here's What to Do...

Weight loss is highly variable from person to person, so the first step you will need to take is to start logging your weight. Weigh yourself in the evening, immediately prior to bedtime and in the morning, immediately after waking and going to the toilet. I would do this every day up until your competition day, starting 7 days out and record every weight for each morning and each night. This will allow you to establish, on average, how much weight you lose overnight (provided you are eating in a stable and consistent manner until competition day).

The Water Load

When I mention "water manipulation" the whole idea is to first "water load", by gradually increasing and then sustaining a higher than usual intake of water for a specific period of time (usually anywhere between 4 and 7 days prior to competition). You are, essentially, overhydrating the body in an attempt to upregulate its water excretion process. You will be pissing like a race horse for these few days, at the end of which, you do a "water cut" and suddenly stop drinking all fluids. The body has a delayed response to this drastic reduction in water consumption and therefore, continues to excrete water from the body at an accelerated pace for some time, even after no more water is being consumed. This does however, leave the body in a slightly dehydrated state.

The cut is where many people make the mistakes. I have seen a lot of protocols that reduce water intake leading up to competition day and completely cut intake far too early. Cutting water early (24 hours or longer away) may be okay for 24-hour weigh-ins since the athlete will have a full 24 hours to rehydrate. However, for 2-hour weigh-ins, one of the keys to stepping on the platform at maximum strength after water loading is to spend as little time in a dehydrated state as possible.

I personally, start the water loading process 5-days out from competition. I have weighed just over 96kg 5 days out and successfully lost over 3kg to weigh-in at under 93kg on competition day after cutting water multiple times without any problem, so I do not see any need to start the process earlier than this. The protocol is very simple but will only work providing you have already been drinking adequate amounts of water in the weeks leading up to beginning the water load. The protocol looks like this:

A Few weeks out: At least 4 Litres of water a day

5 Days out: 6 Litres of water

4 Days out: 8 Litres of water

3 Days out: 8 Litres of water

2 Days out: 10 Litres of water

1 Day out: 10 Litres of water (Cut water i.e. stop drinking all fluids, 12–16 hours before weigh in. For example, if your weigh-in was at 8am you would have to cut all water consumption anytime from 4pm – 8pm).

As I mentioned before, weight loss is very individual and some people may lose water weight and in fact, weight in general, faster than others. If you want to be on the safe side, cutting water 16 hours before weigh-in is likely to give you more weight loss compared to cutting it 12 hours before weigh in. Do bear in mind however, cutting water earlier will lead to a greater degree of dehydration as well as greater weight loss. You will have to find out what works best for you through trial and error until you find the optimum time for you to stop consuming fluids the day before competition.

16.2 AIDS FOR CUTTING WATER

Water loading is the main and most important factor for this rapid reduction in bodily fluids and therefore, body weight to work. For some people, the process will end here; they may easily be able to lose the amount of weight required by simply following the above protocol. There are however, a number of other methods/ techniques that can be employed in addition to water loading to enhance the amount of fluids that are lost after water is cut, which I will outline below. Depending on the individual, you may also need/want to employ some of these additional methods to aid with the excretion of water after the cut. Some methods are harsher on the body than others and, bearing in mind that this information is guided at 2-hour weigh-in, I would not recommend using all of them if you want to maintain your strength as well as make weight.

1) Sodium Manipulation

This is very similar to water manipulation, where you simply increase the amount of sodium you take in to more than your body is used to the week before a meet. This increased sodium intake increases the osmolality in the blood which stimulates the secretion of ADH (an antidiuretic hormone) which results in an increased water reabsorption and retention. As well as aiding water retention initially, the body also begins upregulating the process for metabolizing excess salt. After this "loading phase", sodium is drastically cut in a similar fashion to the water cut. Due to the delayed effect on the body's regulatory mechanism during the loading phase, more water is excreted than usual after sodium is cut. Here is how the sodium protocol goes:

5 Days out: Lightly salt all food (about 5g)

4 Days out: Lightly salt all food (about 5g)

3 Days out: Lightly salt all food (about 5g)

2 Days out: Lower salt (Less than 1g)

1 Day out: No/minimal salt

Although I have outlined the rational for sodium loading and how to cut it, I strongly urge you NOT to use sodium manipulation for a competition with a 2-hour weigh in. I have only used this once in the lead up to competition and I experienced a lot of cramping in various muscles and consider myself very lucky that it did not ruin my competition.

2) Carbohydrate Manipulation

With regards to food manipulation, we are particularly interested in carbohydrates and glycogen levels. The body can store about 400–800g of carbohydrates in the form of glycogen and with every gram of glycogen is stored about 4g of water. So clearly, the more carbohydrates we eat during the water loading phase, the more water our body will hold on to, which is not what we want when trying to expel 3kg of water from our body the day prior to competition. For this reason, I suggest gradually lowering your carbohydrate intake from 6 days out. At this point, the majority of your training sessions should be completed, so this lower intake will not be detrimental. Here is how to gradually lower your carbohydrate intake:

6 Days out (Squat volume singles): Moderate/High Carb

5 Days out (Bench volume singles): Cut normal carb intake by 50% (no more than 200g)

4 Days out: Cut normal carb intake by 75% (no more than 100–150g)

3 Days out: Minimal Carb (calories mainly from protein and healthy fats)

2 Days out: Minimal Carb (calories mainly from protein and healthy fats)

1 Day out: Minimal Carb (calories mainly from protein and healthy fats)

Especially during the minimal carb days, probably also at 4 and 5 days out, you will want to avoid all starchy carbohydrates. Cut out bread, crackers, rice, potatoes, pasta, any products made with dough or flour, and dairy products like cottage cheese, yogurt and cheese. At this point, any carbohydrates should come predominantly from fibrous vegetables such as asparagus, broccoli, leafy greens, and spinach. In addition, with regards to food, I suggest that from 2–3 days out, your last meal of the day be liquid (i.e. a protein shake) as this will accustom your body to having a liquid dinner. Then, on the night before the competition, you should have this final liquid meal 12–16 hours prior to your weigh in, the same time that you cut your water. Having a shake as your last meal before weigh in will ensure that you do not waste precious weight on the scale because you still have food digesting in your system.

As I have continually stressed, everyone is different and their bodies respond differently. The degree to which you need to lower carbohydrates and overall calories during this last week to aid water and weight loss will vary greatly depending on the individual. Again, the best way to find out how much you need to do and how different eating patterns effect your performance is through trial and error and practice before a competition (be sensible about this, you obviously would not want to be experimenting the week before a National or International Championship)!

3) Dehydration/Water Loss Techniques – Sauna and Hot Bath

These techniques are simply used to make you sweat to lose water weight. I have used both of these techniques on occasions. However, saunas and hot baths are risky techniques for cutting weight, especially for 2-hour weigh ins. It is well documented that as little as 2% dehydration can negatively affect performance. Using these methods will expose your body to high temperatures, putting it into a state of dehydration which could potentially compromise your performance on the day. Due to the intermittent nature of powerlifting, this figure of 2% may not be entirely applicable, but nevertheless, I suggest being very conservative with these methods and try to avoid them wherever possible.

If you keep a log of your weight morning and night 5–7 days out, like I previously suggested, you should have a rough idea of how much weight you lose overnight by the time the night before the competition approaches. This will help you to decide whether this last resort method is absolutely necessary. By the time it gets to late evening before you are about to go to bed, if your weight is not within the amount you predict you will lose overnight then you will probably want to get a sweat on in the sauna or a hot bath to lose those last few grams, or dare I say it, last couple of kilos!

For me, I know I like to be within at least 1kg the night before weigh-in to be safe. Therefore, as a 93kg lifter if I am over 94kg late on in the night before I go to bed, I will sweat off a little until I reach my target weight of 94kg.

16.3 When and How to Dehydrate

As previously mentioned, it is essential to spend as little time as possible in a dehydrated state and so the best time to use the sauna or hot bath is as late in the evening as possible. In addition, leaving it as late as possible will mean you are already slightly dehydrated since you will have been peeing for a good few hours. So you will have lost a fair amount of water weight and your stomach will be fairly empty since your last meal should have been liquid and digested pretty quickly. What this means, is that you should already be a long way towards making weight and the amount of water you need to lose via sweating is minimized.

Sauna

Very simply, you sit in the sauna and sweat out the minimum amount of water necessary for you to make weight the following morning or afternoon. Make sure you have scales nearby and after 10–15 minutes in the sauna jump out, dry yourself down and weigh yourself. A method of 10 to 15-min in, 5 to 10-min break and repeat is often utilised. However, one stint of 10 to 15-min should be more than enough. For a 2-hour weigh in, if you need to do more than one stint, you have most probably left yourself with too much to do and will end up feeling weak and very dehydrated the next morning.

Hot Bath

I am well aware that a sauna may not always be accessible, especially if you have had to travel the day before for a competition. I have been in this situation before and find that hot baths work just as well, if not better. I personally prefer a hot bath to a sauna as I can do it in the comfort of my own home or hotel room and I feel that it takes less out of me. Simply fill the bath tub and make it as hot as you can bear it (without burning yourself!). Slowly submerge as much of your body as possible (aside from your head) under the water and stay there for 10 to 20 minutes, then dry yourself down and check your weight. Again, one stint in the bath should be more than enough. In addition to just a hot bath, Epsom salts can also be added to the water which increase its boiling point, thus, allowing you to sweat at a higher temperature than just in hot water alone. Another benefit of using these salts and another reason I favour hot baths over saunas is that the Epsom salts in the bath selectively pull out subcutaneous water (water from under the skin) whereas a sauna non-specifically removes water from the body, which means water can also be removed from the body's organs, making it difficult to rehydrate the next morning. Just simply add 200–400g of the salts to the hot water.

As I mentioned above, these methods are a last resort and it is important to know your limits and not take things too far. Dizziness, nausea, headaches, and tingling are early indicators that you may be over doing it and you should be mindful of these symptoms. If you have to dehydrate yourself to the extent where you experience these symptoms to a severe degree, then chances are you are too heavy anyway and will either not make weight, or will do so at the expense of your strength, health and performance. It is not worth risking your health, or even worse, your life. If you find yourself in this situation, stop the cut, rehydrate, and learn from your mistakes.

16.4 COMPETITION DAY

Morning before the Weigh-In

On the morning of the competition, wake up and go to the toilet. Wherever you are, it is a good idea to have some scales at hand so that you can immediately check your weight after using the toilet and hopefully, you will be right on the money or slightly under. Caffeine is a diuretic and can also have a mild laxative effect. To ensure you get rid of any excess water weight or stool, I would have a strong espresso shot with no water. Even better still would be to take 200 – 400mg of caffeine via tablet form so you do not have to consume any liquid at all. You want to consume absolutely no water before weigh-ins as water is heavy and could potentially undo all of the hard work over the past week.

I also suggest getting to the competition venue as early as you can and check your weight on the competition scales. There is normally some slight variance between your home scales and the ones at competition so it is a good idea to make sure. If you have easily made weight and are a kilo or more under but still have some time before weigh-in, then you can probably afford to start fuelling your body with some calories to start replenishing your muscle glycogen. I would not drink anything before weighing in but it would be safe to slowly start eating some light carbohydrate foods like rice cakes or a cereal bar, for example. At this point, only the actual weight of the food you are eating will affect the number on the scales. So for example, if you weigh 92kg on the competition scales an hour before weigh, you can safely eat 500g worth of food and will weigh in at roughly 92.5kg.

Afternoon Weigh-Ins

If your weigh-in is in the afternoon as opposed to the morning, by and large the above still applies and is relevant. You will just have to adjust certain things slightly to the best of your ability. For example, you will obviously want to cut your water later on in the evening than you would normally do for a morning weigh-in. If you are very close to your competition weight, I would advise still not eating or drinking anything until after the weigh-in, but it would be a good idea to take some form of branch chain amino acid tablets. Only if you are comfortably under the weight you need to be will it be okay to eat a small amount of light weight dry food. Weighing the food before you eat it would also be a sensible idea to give you an indication of how much weight it will add. Much the same as the time you cut your water, if a sauna or hot bath is a necessity, you will want to try and do this as late as possible. Finally, you will want to minimise the time you are awake feeling hungry and thirsty. Therefore, where possible, it is a good idea to stay up and go bed a few hours later than you normally would so that you can wake up slightly later in the morning on competition day.

Post Weigh-in

Congratulations, you have made weight. Now the next two hours immediately post weigh-in are even more important than the week you just spent prepping your body to make weight. Immediately start drinking after you have weighed in. You will have lost a lot of salts and electrolytes over the past 12–16 hours, so I would suggest having a 2-litre bottle of fluid ready made up of 50% plain water and the other %50 some sort of rehydrating electrolyte drink. In terms of electrolyte drinks, Pedialyte is widely recommended, as are coconut water, Gatorade and Powerade. As long as you have something along these lines to dilute with water into a 2-litre bottle I do not think it makes a huge difference. My preference is Pedialyte and coconut water, but the main thing is that before eating anything you consume at least half of this mixture and take one or two mutli-vitamins with it too. This being said, yes you want to rehydrate as much as you can within the 2-hour window, but you do not want to chug 2-litres fluid down as fast as you can or you will risk throwing it straight back up again. Rather, aim to finish at least half of the bottle (1 litre) in 15 to 20 minutes.

After the first 20-mins, once you have consumed at least a litre, start getting food on board. Do not go crazy and start gorging on junk food and sugar that your body is not accustomed to eating. You have just spent the last few days eating a very low amount of carbohydrates and sugar and you do not want to risk becoming hypoglycaemic and suffering from an energy crash. Stick to easy to digest foods that you are used to having on a regular basis. Salty foods are also a good idea. Keep consuming liquids (a mixture of electrolyte drinks and water), at a slightly slower pace to the first litre, right up to before you begin warming up and keep eating until you feel comfortable, but still a little hungry. You do not want to stuff your face so much that you feel full, bloated and like you need go and empty your stomach on the toilet. You will have the whole day to continually eat and, as time goes on, you can start eating and drinking in your more usual manner. You will want to have easily consumed 2-litres, and in some cases closer to 3 or 4-litres by the time lifting commences. I always have foods like liquid carbohydrates and meal replacement or weight gainer shakes (these are quickly absorbed and easy to digest), as well as rice cakes, peanut butter and jam sandwiches, bananas, a couple of baked potatoes with some sachets of salt and a packet of baked, low fat salt and vinegar or ready slated crisps at hand during competitions. I will not consume all of this immediately after the weigh-in, or even before lifting starts, but I know I am used to all of these foods so they will not wreak havoc on my stomach and will eat whatever I fancy from the bunch after drinking, until I feel comfortable. I will also maybe (most highly probably) bring the odd doughnut or 6! I most definitely will not begin eating these directly after weighing-in however. These will be for much later on in the competition, or even just sit there, waiting to be inhaled just seconds after my final deadlift attempt! Some sachets of Dioralyte and rehydration tablets are also always very useful to have on hand, which I will consume as and when needed, diluted with water over the course of the day.

All of the foods I have just listed are what I personally like to consume after weigh in. As I have consistently said, everyone is different and there is no "one size fits all" approach. Food choices will be highly individual and you should stick with whatever you find comfortable and effective.

FINAL COMMENTS

Everything outlined above is close to the exact protocol I have used to make weight successfully and still set PB's in numerous competitions. However, as I have continually stressed, everyone's body is different and will not respond in exactly the same way. What works well for one person may not work so well for another person. The key is to experiment with your own body. What I have outlined for you here is intended only as a guideline or starting point. It is for you take the time to learn and understand your body and tweak certain parts as and when necessary to suit you better. Ensure to first practice these protocols for a mock competition or for a small competition of no significance. Do not use this protocol for the first time before an important Championship, leaving the outcome down to chance. The more times you go through this, the better you will be able to adjust the finer details to fit your body and making weight will become a lot less stressful.

GOOD LUCK!

17

Competition Day Information & Advice

Any good coach will tell you that if you want to build a great total, then you have to hit nine out of nine lifts. If you want to win, do not overshoot. Play it smart.

It is very important to avoid missing your max triples and doubles. Failing at these lifts will only hurt your self-confidence and potentially create too much neuromuscular fatigue. In addition, these misses would make the 1RM Method far less usable for load selection on the all-important day. So as we discussed before, do not overshoot your max triple or double predictor lifts.

You should finish these triples and doubles with confidence, even if the last rep was a hard push, and knowing you have good enough technique that even the strictest of judges will award you the lift. Train the way you compete.

My advice for novice or intermediate lifters is to play it safe and stick with the plan.

Always aim for nine out of nine lifts. Once you gain more experience and are more familiar with competitions, then you can start to experiment and modify your tapering and peaking phases to perhaps enable you to improve your chances of reaching between 2.5–5% higher than your estimated 1RM.

It is very important to always have a plan! That being said, you should always be aware that your 1RM is a dynamic variable which changes from day to day. Always be prepared to change the plan accordingly. The best way to assess what your true 1RM will be on the day of the competition after performing your last warm-up and your first attempt, which should generally be roughly the same weight as your max triple. Then, after your second attempt, you should have all the accurate feedback that you need to make the best possible judgement for the third attempt selection. Whether you are competing for a medal or trying to find your true 1RM "just for fun", the process remains the same.

www.jcconditioning.co.uk instagram / Facebook @jcconditioning

17.1 1RM Method Super-Compensation & Mental Attitude

After two decades of coaching, I have come to understand fully the importance of an effective taper and how this can be literally amplified with a positive mental attitude.

In my experience, lifters following the 1RM Method can achieve, on average, between 2.5–5% increases on their projected 1RM based on their max triple or max double predictor lifts. This percentage is quite normal for the more experienced and *mentally gifted* lifters.

If you are a novice, then I suggest sticking to the plan and using your max triple and max double predictor lifts to estimate your 100% 1RM attempt. However, as you become more accomplished, you can rightfully assume that you will gain an increase between 2.5–5% based on your predictor lifts.

93kg 2015 Senior British champion Pierre Shillingford, 57kg 2014–2015 M1 British champion 2015 IPF World silver medallist Pelin Baykal, Me with the first ever IPF World Seniors classic team trophy, 93kg Juniors 2013–2014–2015 champion 2015 EPF European champion Sion Hughes.

For example, your max triple will usually be around 90–93% of your 1RM and a technically sound max double will usually fall between 94–97% of your 1RM. So, let's say that you perform a 200kg squat for a max double predictor lift and you then assume the lifted weight to be about 95% of your 1RM. As a result, you are, essentially, predicting your new 1RM to be an increase of 5%, giving you a new weight of 210kg for the squat on the day of the championship. Well, in many cases, what you will find by effectively performing the 1RM Method taper and peak systems, is the creation of a super-compensation effect. As a result, you are far more likely to achieve an extra 2.5% on top of your estimated 5%, giving you a new overall increase of an extra 7.5% for your 1RM potential.

If everything goes according to plan, then your new estimated squat weight will rise from 210kg to a whopping 215kg on the day of the competition. As you become more accustomed to the 1RM Method, you can have some fun experimenting with this concept. Remember, we are all very different from powerlifter to powerlifter and we all adapt to training stimuli very differently. So it is always best to play it safe for the first few times that you run through this method until you become more accustomed to how your body responds.

Now, I am no sports psychologist, but I have worked alongside several with my athletes over the years. As a result, I have truly come to believe that having the correct psychological approach to lifting makes a world of difference in competitive powerlifting, especially at the elite-levels of the sport.

It is a good idea to spend about five minutes after every training session positively visualising all of the successful attempts that you *will make* at the next coming championship. However, never mentally imagine lifting just before you sleep because what often happens instead is that the extra excitement tends to only increase the heart rate and adrenaline production. This is not a good recipe for achieving the high-quality sleep that you want, especially on the night before a competition.

I recommend to all my lifters and athletes to only perform visualisation exercises at prescribed times. Your goal is to avoid thinking about the upcoming championship all week long, 24/7, as your body will just perceive this as a form of stress. As we said earlier, over and over again, your body does not care whether your stress comes from training or everyday life. Any form of stress will only increase the heart rate and cortisol levels through the sympathetic nervous system, which ultimately leads to a substantial decrease in your ability to recover fully and maximise strength between sessions or peak.

17.2 General Advice: Preparing to Compete

When preparing for a competition, be prepared, because no lifter ever gets everything right all at once, regardless previous competitive experience. Obviously you are far more likely to come closer to your goals with a team of reputable and dedicated coaches and assistant coaches helping you.

You may as well get used to the fact that the chances are, everything will not always go according to plan on the day, so just let it go! Do not dwell on it! Instead, focus on what you *can* do on your next attempt or lift. You will have plenty of time afterwards to acknowledge your mistakes. Then simply commit to learning from them for the next event.

Focus on the here and now – take one lift at a time!
Championships are nearly always won by the lifter who achieves the most successful attempts. So do not think about the past *or* the future. Think in the now! Focus on what you have to do to "get the job done" at this moment in time, not just about winning or losing.

When you are in between warm-ups or competitive lifts and have a few spare minutes, use your visualisation skills to imagine yourself successfully achieving the lift while maintain perfect form and technique. However, take care not to psych yourself up too much; not yet anyway. Save that aggression and determination for when it counts during your turn on the platform at the competition.

The real trick for beginners is to still maintain cognitive awareness so that you hear the commands without totally zoning out. Believe in yourself! Do not place limits on your abilities and you too, can achieve great things!
Every individual rep that you perform using the 1RM Method should be able to pass the scrutiny of the strictest referees. My suggestion, film every rep and review the video with your team for both strengths *and* weaknesses. After all, you are usually your own worst critic.

Filming every lift that you perform over 80% of your 1RM is a must, especially if you do not have good coach and sometimes even if you do. To be totally blunt, I have seen too many bad coaches telling their lifters, "Great Lift!" or "Well done!" even though the lift was clearly miles off and the technique totally sucked! It never hurts to film everything so that you can review your technique and lifting style yourself, anytime that you want!

Also, do not get sucked into *"Going Hollywood"* when creating your YouTube or Facebook videos. There are loads of lifters out there who are considered "social media sensations" and who all the other lifters automatically assume are going to hit huge totals and win championships. In actual fact, for most of these "wannabe champions", they can never seem to live up to their self-generated media hype. For one thing, many of these lifters tend to manipulate the camera angles to hide many of their flaws. They are only interested in showing off and only pay attention to what they are doing *right* while trying to ignore what they are doing *wrong*. *Long term gains are made from correcting what is wrong, not ignoring it.*

Do not forget our motto, "If you fail to plan, you plan to fail".
If you plan well for your upcoming championship, then you will rarely fail. Yes, sometimes unexpected obstacles in life for which you could have never possibly have planned, like a nightmare at work or a few nights

of bad sleep due to a sick child do occasionally pop up. This is okay. Just hit the gym, but drop a rep from the sets that are giving you the most trouble and to get as close as you can on the day to the desired minimum volume threshold required. If you are so stressed and so tired that you are even starting to grind on singles, then you might want to listen to your body and call it a day. Give it your best shot once you are better recovered. After all, you may be a badass powerlifter, but you are still only human.

17.3 Visualisation Exercises

The power of the mind is simply incredible and having a healthy level of self-belief and confidence (not arrogance) in one's abilities is the most valuable asset that you can bring to any competition. In many, many ways, self-esteem plays an even more important role in winning and achieving your ultimate 1RM on the all-important day.

Let's say that you are looking at 300kg on your third and final attempt. To date, your best max double is only 285kg and your best 1RM in competition is 290kg from about four months ago. It takes incredible strength-of-mind to believe that all of your training and long hours in the gym has successfully set you up for this incredible moment in time. If you truly believe that you can do it, then chances are that you will!

There must be no doubt in your mind that you can make your next lift. This is how a true champion always thinks; win, lose, or draw!

Powerlifters must be strong physically *and* mentally. One of the things I love the most about powerlifting is the diversity of people that gravitate to this sport. I have coached many young athletes over the years who first came to me as shy, introverted individuals. Through the sport of powerlifting and the related visualisation techniques, a very large portion eventually build a healthy self-esteem and self-confidence that translated from the gym into nearly all areas of their personal and professional life.

An example of a ritual for success in the squat

Here is the protocol that I use as a professional coach to set up each lift. I always allow each lifter to put their own personal spin on each lift as well, to instil a sense of ownership and create a sense of personal ritual as they temporarily transition from "my lifter" to "their own man/woman in charge of his/her own destiny".

Example: A Successful Squat

1. Walk up to the rack loaded at 100% of your 1RM. Let the psychological arousal begin to take over.
2. Grip the bar firmly and properly. Meanwhile, the bar should be at approximately mid-sternum level but facing your face.
3. Step under the bar and lift the elbows to accommodate the bar position on the spine of the scapular while also lifting your rib cage, effectively trapping the bar in a solid position.
4. Brace every single muscle fibre possible throughout the entire body and lift. At this point, your psychological arousal should be between 96–98%.
5. Next, inhale deeply to activate the Valsalva manoeuvre.
6. You should un-rack the bar by performing a partial squat. This is not only the safest way, but it will also serve to prime the neuromuscular system for what you are about to lift through a full range of movement.
7. Only take three steps backward from the rack to set up your squat. This minimises any potential energy loss useful for achieving the lift. Also, you can still breathe, or at least breathe shallowly, while setting up. You do not want pass out right before lift. You want to be self-confident and ready to display your new maximal strength and a new Personal Best!
8. Once you are in your perfect set position to squat, look purposefully at the centre referee to acknowledge your readiness. Then wait for his or her command. When the command is given, take your final deep

breath. This very last deep breath is your cue to ramp up to 100% psychological arousal while holding everything as tight as humanly possible. *Now attack the lift!*

"There is only you and the bar. Nothing can stop you from making depth and driving the hips and chest upward. Nothing can stop you from achieving this lift!"

18

Interviews from the world's Elite level lifters and What They do the Day before a Competition

18.1 Ray Orlando Williams

Year of Birth: 1986

Current Weight Class: Super heavy weight 120+kg

Years competing: 4 years (2012-present)

Nationality: US

Instagram: @optimusprime_334

Facebook: Ray Williams Powerlifting

Personal bests and records

Best Competition Squat: 438kg (965.6lbs) [World record]

Best Competition Bench Press: 245kg (540.1lbs)

Best Competition Deadlift: 365kg (803lbs)

Best Competition Total: 1,043kg (2299.4lbs) [World Record]

1. Please list your biggest championship achievements:
IPF World Classic Champion 2014, 2015 & 2016.

2. Of your biggest championship achievements which one means the most to you and why?
That would be my very first championship that I won at the IPF Open Raw Championship in South Africa. It was special because I was not 100% healthy, I had to fight through losing 25 pounds traveling to the meet and I had other adversities to deal with as well. This championship showed me that if you just keep fighting and remain relentless, you can conquer anything.

3. What would you class as your biggest errors prior to a championship?
Not being mentally prepared to compete.

4. How have you rectified those errors?
As a lifter, now when it is time to compete, I lock in on the competition and the competition only. I am one of those people, I may take in the sights and all that after my meet, but I like to mentally prepare myself for the mental and physical strain that comes with powerlifting.

5. What one thing would you say has had the most impact on your successful preparation?
Having two great gyms close by that I have 24-hours access to. Power Zone Gym and It awamba Community College Fitness Centre. If I want to work on my technique I have the freedom to go to the gym as early, or as late as I need to.

6. Do you have any specific do's and don'ts 24 hours before a big championship?
Do's: Rest and to take as many naps as I can in a day, get as many massages as I can in a day, eat as much rice and pasta as I can get and hydrate as much as possible.

Don'ts: I normally try to stay off my cell phone, I don't walk around too much, avoid any type of caffeine enriched produces, and I stay away from greasy or fried foods; no bacon or pork because of the fact that they raise your blood pressure.

7. How do you deal with pre-competition nerves 24 hours before and on the day of the competition?
Well the day of the meet is very important because, after weigh-ins, I become very anti-social. I isolate myself away from people as much as possible and just listen to my music and try to stay as calm as possible. The day before is easy; I am as lazy as possible and talk to and enjoy my family as much as I can.

8. Do you have any nutritional advice after making weight on the day of the competition?
I normally don't eat anything after weigh-in because I typically eat a really good, clean breakfast. Most of the time in big competitions the Super heavy weight class competes in the noon, so I will still be full from breakfast.

9. How do you deal with the unexpected on the day of the championship?
I have one of the best supporting casts in the world. For example, on the day of the Championship in South Africa, when I was about to warm up, I noticed that my knee sleeves were smaller than normal. Then I realized that I had packed my elbow sleeves, but didn't panic. I found an SBD representative and they got me a brand new pair of knee sleeves to compete in. This kind of thing happens all the time and at this past championship in Finland, SBD just supplied me with an extra pair of everything just in case I left something behind. Lastly, with

the support of my coaches and family, it is easy when you look in the audience and someone that you love is out there smiling at you.

10. How do you mentally prepare the day of a competition?
I zone out, clear my mind and only think about what it is that I am there to do. Right before I start my warm-ups, I take a knee, thank God for the opportunity and give it all I have because, in the end, all the glory is his.

11. What do you focus on in between attempts and disciplines during a competition?
Matt and Sioux-z Gary (US Team Coaches) do a great job thinking for me at most of my meets. I listen to their feedback and ideas that would make me more efficient as a lifter. The main thing is staying in my zone. I have to stay focused on the mission at hand until the competition is over.

12. Can you describe your mental process prior to going to the platform?
It is organized chaos. When I take the platform I am very animated and very hyped because I train very hard, as do all the other lifters. When you take the platform, that is your time to dominate, I take it to the highest levels and give it all I got. That way when I turn around and await those lights to come on, if I get the outcome I want, I feel absolutely fulfilled that everything that I have worked for has come to fruition.

18.2 Owen Hubbard

Year of birth: 1992

Current Weight class: 83kg

Years competing: 8 at present

Nationality: Great Britain

Website: www.owenhubbardfitness.com

Instagram: @ohubb

Personal bests and records

Best Competition Squat: 271kg (596.2lbs) – [British & European senior record]

Best Competition Bench: 205kg (451lbs)– [British Record]

Best Competition Deadlift: 277.5kg (610.5lbs)

Best Competition Total: 748.5kg (1646.7lbs)

1. Please list your biggest championship achievements

Becoming junior Commonwealth, European and World champion all in the same year, as well as breaking the senior world record bench as a junior. Most recently, I am very proud of achieving silver in my first international as a senior. Taking that step up is a big thing for a lot of lifters, so to be competitive as a senior so young is a great feeling.

2. Of your biggest championship achievements which one means the most to you and why?

This has got to be winning the Junior Worlds in Finland. After squatting 270kg and benching 205kg I was in a strong position but failed my second deadlift after going into full body cramp and had to be carried off the stage. This gave the guys below me a sniff at pinching the win so I knew I had to pull my third to close out that chance. I walked on, still in cramp, and pulled 270kg in the most compromised position of all time to stop myself from cramping further. Somehow it stuck and I walked away with the win. How I managed to pull it off I will never know, but I will always remember that for sure.

3. What would you class as your biggest errors prior to a championship?

Not listening to my body and eventually overtraining leading up to the Commonwealth Championships. This was my last year as a junior and I had been doing competition after competition and not getting any stronger. This was a big mistake. I got really fatigued and over-trained and really didn't get stronger for a whole six months.

4. How have you rectified those errors?

I've started to auto-regulate my training a lot more, which has really helped. I used to have set days, set percentages and set working sets I would work to no matter what, but now I have really benefited from accepting that I cannot keep smashing the wall 24/7 and expect to push through a plateau. I no longer worry about the odd missed session if I am feeling a bit fried or fatigued. I would much rather one productive session than two half arsed ones.

5. What one thing would you say has had the most impact on your successful preparation?

Just solid programming and always keeping an open mind to every single peak. I will sit down with my coach and look back on what has happened in the previous cycle and see how we can create an even more effective peak next time. I am a true believer in trial and error, always adapting programmes to promote a change.

6. Do you have any specific *do's and don'ts* 24 hours before a big championship?

I would say try and stay away from anything that is lifting-based as much as you can, it will panic you and just wear you down. Personally I just try to keep myself busy but distance myself quite a bit from what is going to happen in a day's time. At internationals, that usually means just relaxing in my hotel room, going for a short walk, or just watching mindless foreign TV! At home I tend to like to just keep the day as normal as possible and work, if I can, get home and get an early night ready for the big day ahead.

7. How do you deal with pre-competition nerves 24 hours before and on the day of the competition?

I'm quite methodological with this; I think it is the structure that calms me. The night before I will empty out my kit back and repack it, I will go to sleep, wake up and then do the exact same thing. Don't know why, maybe just in case someone has stolen my stuff overnight? Then in the morning I will shower and do all the standard stuff of getting my bag ready (again) and ensuring I have literally everything I need. Once I have weighed in, refuelled and started warming up I see the small amount of nerves as a good thing and use them to my advantage. The way I think of it is that I can't change anything at this point, so why worry about if it's all going to be fine on the day.

8. Do you have any nutritional advice after making weight on the day of the competition?

Rehydrating and refuelling as quickly as possible is the key to performance on the day. You want to be doing this straight when you get off the scales and not 10 minutes later when you've collected your stuff, put your attempts in and repacked your bag up. After this then just stick to light, carbohydrate rich meals but not massively high in sugars from the word go. I tend to find this is the mistake lots of people make. You've spent a week or so being depleted from these and getting a big hit of glucose all at once is just going to send you to sleep. If you have sugars early, you have to keep them consistently high throughout the competition. Therefore, I much prefer keeping to complex carbohydrates straight after weigh in and then ingesting more sugary foods later on in the day.

9.How do you deal with the unexpected on the day of the championship?

I think if something goes wrong or not quite how you expect it to at the time, accept it and move on. The worst thing you can do is get caught up in it because most of the time this snowballs into the whole competition becoming a flop. Personally, I think this is where a good support team comes in and where coaches and teammates really come into their own. They can help with a lot of the background stuff that might get you flustered but isn't worth it.

10. How do you mentally prepare the day of a competition?

When I start to warm up I like to be organised and I always set times that I will do each and every warm up to ensure that I am on time for my opening lift. During this time, I don't really become mentally focused until the last one or two warm ups. If anyone has seen me lift, I am quite animated so if I were to put that intensity in all the way though the comp I wouldn't even make it to the bench, never mind all the way through!

During the competition, music does a lot for me. I have a few playlists for different times of the day, whether it is before I've started lifting, during warm ups or in between lifts. There are a handful of songs that are a trigger to lifting heavy, and I keep these for competition (and the odd heavy gym session).

Top 5 lifting songs (if anyone is interested)

1. Drowning Pool – Bodies

2. Rob Bailey & The Hustle Standard – Try 'n Hold Me Back

3. Beartooth – Body Bag

4. System of a Down – B.Y.O.B

5. Slipknot – Custer

11. What do you focus on in between attempts and disciplines during a competition?

Just the next lift and nothing else. I try to envisage a successful lift over and over in my head until I hear the words *"bar is loaded"*, then I'm ready to go. That's all that matters on the day.

Between disciplines I tend to try and come down a little and relax a bit.

12. Can you describe your mental process prior to going to the platform?

I will give myself a bit of a pep talk under my breath, but apart from that it's just going out there and lifting it and not over complicating things. In the warm up room, the gym and on the platform I make every lift as identical to each other as I can, which is why I have some quite elaborate set ups on all 3 lifts! Every single part of my set up on all lifts is for a reason and is actually a cue to prepare myself for the lift. Elaborate set ups for the sake of it are just a waste of energy in my opinion.

18.3 Kimberly C. Walford

Year of Birth: 1978

Current Weight Class: 72kg

Years competing: 14

Nationality: US

Instagram: @trackfu

Facebook: Kimberly C. Walford

Personal bests and records

Best Competition Squat: 186kgs (410lbs) [American Record]

Best Competition Bench Press: 115kgs (253lbs)

Best Competition Deadlift: 242.5kgs (534.6lbs) [World Record], [American Record]

Best Competition Total: 540kgs (1190.49lbs) [World Record], [American Record]

1. Please list your biggest championship achievements:
- 4x IPF Classic World Champion (Open 63kg 2012/2013, 72kg classes 2014/2015)
- Broken 16 Open, classic world records
- Multi time U.S. National champion and American record holder

2. Of your biggest championship achievements which one means the most to you and why?
Winning the 2013 IPF Classic 63kg championship because I faced adversity in the bench press. I missed the first two lifts on technical call and it came down to the third attempt to stay in the competition.

3. What would you class as your biggest errors prior to a championship?
Underestimating the power of travel and how it can negatively affect weight loss during meet week.

4. How have you rectified those errors?

Eat extra carbs meet week up to the night before competition, ensure I get sufficient rest, stay hydrated and arrive into the international country at least two days prior to competing.

5. What one thing would you say has had the most impact on your successful preparation?

Versatility, learning and adapt to become as efficient and effective as you can in training and on the platform.

6. Do you have any specific do's and don'ts 24 hours before a big championship?

Do get enough sleep, rest, and, nutrients. Don't allow stress and any negativity take you off your game.

7. How do you deal with pre-competition nerves 24 hours before and on the day of the competition?

I remind myself how hard I've worked to prepare for competition day. Sometimes I sequester myself to my hotel room or a peaceful place to clear my head and mentally prepare for the platform.

8. Do you have any nutritional advice after making weight on the day of the competition?

Carb up and hydrate immediately after you step off the weighing scale.

9. How do you deal with the unexpected on the day of the championship?

You adapt, it's all I feel you can do to prepare for unexpected events.

10. How do you mentally prepare the day of a competition?

My mental prep includes sufficient sleep, visualization of aspects of training and warm ups/competition attempts, prayer, and listening to my "game day" music list.

11. What do you focus on in between attempts and disciplines during a competition?

I focus on staying hydrated, sufficient nutrition and my plan for each attempt. No excess movement, if not doing warm ups, attempts, or bathroom breaks I stay in my "zone" within the warm up area.

12. Can you describe your mental process prior to going to the platform?

I'm 100% committed mentally and physically, "let's do this"!

18.4 Stephen Manuel

Year of Birth: 1988

Current Weight Class: 105kg

Years competing: 10

Nationality: Great Britain

Instagram: @screamermanuel

Personal bests and records

Best Competition Squat: 325kgs (716.5lbs) [National Record]

Best Competition Bench Press: 207.5kgs (457.4lbs)

Best Competition Deadlift: 325kgs (715lbs)

Best Competition Total: 837.5kgs (1846.3lbs) [National Record]

1. Please list your biggest championship achievements
- Gold medal squat in the 2013 World Championships
- Silver medal overall in the 2013 World Championships
- Won 9 British Championships and held over 30 British Records in the GBPF
- Top 3 at World Championships for the last three years (2013–2015) across two different weight classes

2. Of your biggest championship achievements which one means the most to you and why?
There are two that stand out for me. First is my Gold medal squat (and actually the overall performance) from 2013. I was a huge underdog in 2013 as it was my first International Classic competition – I was only just nominated in the top 10 and nobody knew who I was. After losing out on the World title on the final deadlift (in all fairness, I was never going to pull that weight but I had 2nd place secured, so I went for what I needed) and breaking out as the best squatter in the division that year, I felt I had arrived where I belonged, at the top end of the sport. That also, would prove to be my downfall in future as well.

The next year I had a lot of expectations on me from fans of the sport and I was going well in training for the British Championships (2013). Then I was involved in car crash one week out from the competition. I had done my opening weights for the competition that very day, I forget the bench and deadlift numbers but I squatted an easy 270kg. After the crash I tried squatting on the Monday and couldn't hit depth with 40kg. Talk about a Mind F**k, right?! I finished 3rd that year in the 93kg class and honestly, I was devastated and this made me question my future in the sport. I saw myself as a failure, despite being seriously injured, coming through rehab, hitting a PB total and medalling at Worlds all in the space of 8 months.

The second achievement which means the most to me is my Bronze medal from last year's World Championships (2015) and the reason for this is two-fold. One, because I moved up a division to the 105kg class and also because of how happy I was to achieve this and not actually take the win. It was a huge indicator that I was maturing as a person and as a lifter that in only a year I went from putting enormous pressure on myself and being upset with finishing 3rd in the world to being proud of my accomplishments with the same result in a tougher field.

3. What would you class as your biggest errors prior to a championship?
Up until the European Championships of this year (where I got drunk two days out and banned from the competition), I don't feel I made any errors prior to a Championships. I have a certain set of fundamentals that I stick to: not going off plan in training, packing my things nice and early so I have time to do my double and triple checks without pressure, I watch superhero movies the night before, I try not to change anything about the routine because it's mine and makes me comfortable; but I do stick to a routine.

4. What one thing would you say has had the most impact on your successful preparation?
Trusting the process and knowing that the hard work is done. Too many people want to fail stuff all the time and this is the reason why you see them failing at competitions. They're either used to failing lifts, or making glaring technical errors (like not hitting depth in squats) because they have been training so heavy they're apprehensive about sitting competition deep.

Train how you compete, and compete how you train!

5. Do you have any specific *dos and don'ts* 24 hours before a big championship?

Not really, other than what I highlighted before. My best advice is to try to get as much rest as possible and do things that you would normally do to limit the stress and anxiety – something I wish I'd done in Estonia. Just chill out, watch TV and don't be afraid to be quiet around people, it's understandable and your team will be there for you.

6. How do you deal with pre-competition nerves 24 hours before and on the day of the competition?

I'm usually nervous right up until I get the first squat on the platform done. So the day before can be pretty bad, but I try not to change my routine too much if I can help it. If I'm back home, I'll work up until the early afternoon as this helps takes my mind off it and then I watch my Superhero movies (specifically Batman and Superman stuff). I weigh myself before bed as a habit and if I'm only 1–1.5kg over I know I'm set and that's one less thing to worry about.

7. Do you have any nutritional advice after making weight on the day of the competition?

There's no magical food or drink that's going to add 50kg to your total, so don't even bother trying to find out. Just eat the things you like and more importantly, that don't unsettle your stomach. Some people find it hard to eat because of the nerves so it's always good to have some meal replacement drinks on hand to still be able to get calories in.

Although in the grand scheme of things you're not actually breaking that much muscle tissue with a typical competition day, it's still a long time to have no calories coming in so have plan A (food) and plan B (liquid calories) and then you can't go wrong.

8. How do you deal with unexpected on the day of the championship?

I do this at regional and national competitions. I run the numbers myself and load my own bars (not so much at the British) so I have no choice but to be stressed and deal with potential screw ups regularly in the year. Then when I get to International competitions and the head coach and coaching staff are there it's a welcome break from all of that stuff and I just put my trust in those guys to keep me right so I can listen to my metal and scream my face off.

I have great belief in myself and even in the event of any unwanted stress I know I'm still one of the best out there. As an example, I entered a regional competition as a 105kg lifter and then weighed in at 106kg and didn't bother to drop the weight as I was on my way down for a bigger competition and didn't want the stress. Unbeknownst to me, this changed my grouping and I ended up lifting with the guest lifters in the group before the 105kg class – I found this out 10 minutes before lift-off and hadn't started warming up. So I went 70, 120, 170, 220 in the space of 5 minutes and then hit 260 as my final warm up after another 5 minutes and then went and competed. I hit a 310 squat that day and it was very comfortable. The point is, when shit happens there's no point in getting wound up – just get on with it and do your best. I was prepared for big lifts that day and I didn't stress over not making weight or the mess up with the timing, I just got to work and hit a Personal Best overall.

9. How do you mentally prepare the day of a competition?

I try to stay as scheduled as I can. I can be a little stand offish on competition days, I don't mean to be rude, but that's just how I can come across. I try to divert the topic of conversation away from "what are you aiming for today?" – funnily enough what everyone asks you, it's like Powerlifter Tourette's. I don't like making big claims about the lifts I'll get because I am a little superstitious about that stuff I guess. I just let my performance do the talking.

10. What do you focus on in between attempts and disciplines during a competition?

Honestly, I mess around in the back! I love to have a laugh so I'm cracking jokes and being my usual boisterous self. At the same time, turning up the intensity is like flipping the lights on. I can go from laughing my head off to screaming the house down in seconds.

11. Can you describe your mental process prior to going to the platform?

OK. So I like to see the bar being loaded. Every plate that gets added just gets me that more excited and the longer it takes the better because I get very impatient because all I want to do is go and own that bar. I never break eye contact with the bar.

Just writing this is making my heart rate increase dramatically! Have you ever seen that film Unleashed with Jet Li, where they keep him locked up until he is going to fight in a cage and they unlock his collar and he just goes ACKA on everybody! That's me when I hear "Bar is loaded" I steam towards the bar, go to the far side of the bar, eyeing up my prey and checking there isn't a misload (this has happened at a competition before so I always double check now), then I come to the near side and do the same, then I go to the middle for one last look my objective – then the scream comes out. I find the scream makes me tingle and puts me at that perfect point of arousal where I'm so fired up nothing can stop me now!

Then when the scream has come in the technical stuff comes out to play. "Are my hands in the right place?", "have I put the bar in the right place on my back?", "are my feet in the right place?" etc. It's like a NASA systems check before a launch, but I can't do that efficiently without all the nonsense beforehand to clear my mind! Then once the systems check is done, it's time to do the damn thing – this part is obviously very technical but I don't have to think of anything about how I lift because I spend so much time on technique it is just second nature now. It's easier than walking – genuinely!

19

fundamental Mechanics of a Competition Squat, Bench, And Deadlift.

I often revisit these fundamentals, even with my more advanced lifters. You will be surprised at how quickly those old bad habits can creep back into your lifting and corrupt your technique. By paying attention to the fundamentals below, you will stay on track and keep improving month after month, year after year.

Please beware. If you suffer from high blood pressure or any other medical conditions, you should always consult your doctor before performing any lifting.

19.1 The Squat

We should all learn, or at least revisit, the fundamentals of a proper squat. This is just a blueprint, but as you gain more experience under the guidance of a good coach, you might make some adjustments and slightly manipulate the mechanics, if needed.

- **Step One:** To perform a good quality raw powerlifting style squat, your feet should be at a width that is only slightly wider than the hips for increased stability and to accommodate the torso travelling between the knees to achieve depth.
- **Step Two:** Once you place your feet at this width, look down your leg to your patella (knee cap) and adjust the feet to align at the same angle as your patella. This will normally mean pointing your feet outward by approximately 15–20 degrees. This position will minimise any sheer force and allow correct mechanics of the knee joint as you drop to the ideal depth.
- **Step Three:** Rack height is very important. First, simply walk up to the bar and rack so that it is at the approximate height of your sternum. This next part may sound trivial, but it is very important. Once the bar has enough loaded weight, it will act as the centre of mass and if the centre of mass is not positioned correctly on your back, then everything else will be wrong too.
- **Step Four:** For the positioning of the hands on the bar, I always recommend taking as narrow a grip as your frame and flexibility will allow. This position will accommodate the tightest possible upper back during the squat.
- **Step Five:** Now, duck under the bar, placing the bar below the spine of the scapula. Next, tighten all the muscles in the thoracic spine so that the weight of the bar is supported by, not crushing down on, the skeletal system.
- **Step Six:** I generally recommend taking a thumb-less/false grip on the bar, as this will essentially encourage the lifter to raise the elbows and keep wrists straight, which is very important for a number of reasons. Firstly, by lifting the elbows and maintaining a straight wrist position, it will be highly unlikely that you will

unintentionally try to support much of the bar's weight on your wrists, elbows, and shoulder joints. As a result, you reduce the chances of possible injuries that are common among powerlifters who align their elbows directly below the bar. Secondly, lifting the elbow will trap the bar between the back and the chest, creating the most stable lifting position. Thirdly, lifting the elbows will generally encourage a lower bar position, which is ideal for max effort lifting. Lastly, lifting the elbows along with tilting the head down will encourage the optimal torso angle to recruit the most from glutes and hamstrings while performing a squat using maximal loads.

- **Step Seven:** It is important when squatting maximal loads to activate the Valsalva manoeuvre. In doing so, the core acts as a non-compressible cylinder, increasing overall stability and allowing the lifting of greater loads. There has been a great deal of scientific research showing that the Valsalva manoeuvre also has the potential to increase neural drive. As a general rule, I almost always see lifters do this instinctively when exposed to larger loads, but if for some reason the lifter does not automatically start to use the Valsalva manoeuvre when loads increase, then as their coach, I will simply ask them to take a deep breath and compress their diaphragm while activating all of the abdominals.

- **Step Eight:** To achieve the proper positioning of the pelvis, I usually ask my lifters to focus on maintaining a slight anterior tilt throughout the squat. For most lifters, this is the hardest thing to get right, especially when you are about to break depth. Your pelvis will want to be forced into a posterior tilt unless you fight like crazy with your lower back musculature to maintain the anterior tilt position. It is very important to avoid the posterior tilt at all costs for a number of reasons. Firstly, your spine is not as strong when positioned with a posterior, compared to an anterior tilt. So you will likely not lift as much when using a posterior tilt position compared to when you adopt an anterior tilt position. By trying with everything you have got to maintain the anterior tilted pelvis position, you are more likely to achieve a neutral positioning of the spine, which is the safest and optimal position for squatting maximal loads. The second reason is a very important one if you want to lift as much weight as possible. If you allow your pelvis to tuck under and go into a posterior titled position, then you are effectively reducing the crucial stretch-shortening cycle, which is phenomenally important to create drive out of the hole. If this happens, then the stretch-shortening cycle will not be as efficient at recruiting from the big muscle groups like the glutes and hamstrings, all of which will significantly reduce your ability to lift maximal loads.

- **Step Nine:** The weight distribution should be placed at about mid-foot or slightly towards the heel of the foot. Your feet should always be slightly wider than hip-width apart to better recruit the glutes. You can also focus on keeping the weight distribution towards the outside of the foot, but when doing so, be sure that the knees always track directly over your feet.

- **Step Ten:** Before beginning the lift, tilt the head down slightly until you are looking at the floor about 5 feet in front of you. This is also very important for a number of reasons. The first was explained earlier regarding the correct torso angle. The second reason is very simple, but very, *VERY* important when lifting in competitions. By looking about 5-feet in front of you, you get constant feedback and reference so that you will be better prepared to squat using any of the squat racks at your gym. You will also be far better prepared to squat at any championship. To put this another way, looking 5-feet in front will give you the ideal feedback needed for promoting better kinaesthetic awareness, allowing you to lift maximal loads properly using any rack, in any location around the world.

- **Step Eleven:** Initiate the squatting movement from the hip. I generally coach my lifters to break from the hip gradually, pushing their hips backward throughout the eccentric part of the lift. This is important for a number of reasons too. By pushing backward, you place more emphasis on the larger muscle groups, like the glutes and hamstrings. Second, by pushing backward, you create a more 90-degree shin angle, which means that you achieve ideal squat depth sooner and with less wasted movement.

- **Step Twelve:** Forcefully drive up from the hip to finish the movement, it is very important to maintain your torso angle until the last 25% of the squat. By maintaining this angle, you keep the emphasis on recruiting from larger muscle groups.

19.2 The Bench

The bench is where you should be especially placing 110% effort on holding a tight position, even during the warm-up sets. The fundamentals of this exercise begin with the retraction of your scapula with your rhomboids before lifting from the rib cage. Focus all of your effort on using your lats to assist depressing the scapula while focusing on externally rotating the humerus, your elbows will drop down slightly, which will better accommodate the fixed scapula position created by the bench.

Okay. Let's start from the top.

- **Step One:** We will begin by focusing on the proper arch. The easiest and most repeatable way to set up a bridge and to create a good arch, is by placing your feet at the end of the bench while lifting your pelvis to the highest possible position. There are a few very good reasons as to why you want to create the biggest possible arch for a competition bench.

    The first and most obvious reason, is the reduced range of movement that the bar has to travel with a maximised, proper arch. Secondly, by creating a larger arched position, you are essentially placing yourself in a more mechanically advantageous position to move heavier loads. This is because the line of force better matches the gross muscle pennation angles of the Pecs and delts. The third reason, and probably the least well-known, is that a proper arch will allow the lats to better assist the rotator cuff musculature in the stabilisation of the glenohumeral joint. In doing so, a reduction of inhibitory signals sent to prime movers occurs, which allows you to lift greater loads more safely.

- **Step Two:** The feet should always be placed flat on the floor, which significantly reduces the chances of your feet slipping. Most importantly, it is one of the very strict rules of competition powerlifting at elite level. Place the feet flat on the floor, moderately wide apart, to create lateral stability for the hips and to transfer tightness throughout the entire lifting position. You will also want to bring the feet as far back towards the hips as possible, creating an acute angle at the knee joint. This position helps constant drive from the legs so maintain the bridged position more effectively. When setting up for this position, your ultimate goal is to keep the weight displacement over the upper shoulders as much as possible, fighting to avoid any possible loss of position.

- **Step Three:** The grip position is somewhat unique to the individual powerlifter. As long as it is not wider than 81 cm, then your grip will be within the rules of competitive lifting.

- **Step Four:** For the proper, overall body position on the high-quality benches, you focus your eyesight directly below the bar. This position allows for minimal movement and effort to un-rack the bar, even when assisted by a spotter. The proper body position also helps maintain the proper arch and the related tightness that is so crucial for achieving maximal lifts.

- **Step Five:** Next, un-rack the bar and locate the position of least effort for holding the load. This will always be your start position. Again, retract your scapular with your rhomboids. Then lift the rib cage before focusing all of your effort on using your lats to assist depressing the scapula. Intuitively, your humerus should externally rotate basically your elbow will rotate inward, which is what you want.

- **Step Six:** Now it is time to take a deep breath and activate the Valsalva manoeuvre. Inhale deeply before you even begin the rep, which will allow for a more complete filling of the lungs, a better chest angle and more stability for increased force to be applied to the bar.

- **Step Seven:** Now, only now, you will drop your pelvis to the bench while keeping your butt just touching the bench. It is very important to remember that all of the real weight displaced will be on your upper back and shoulders. There should be very little weight being transferred through your pelvis to the bench, or you will likely begin to lose that perfect arch.

- **Step Eight:** The legs contribute considerably in a bench press. They create an applied force in a predominately horizontal plane, force that is useful in maintaining as much weight displacement as possible through the upper back and shoulders. There is also a small amount of vertical force from the legs that is used for maintaining the biggest possible bridge while simultaneously keeping your glutes in contact with the bench.

- **Step Nine:** The ultimate goal when lowering the bar to the chest during the bench press is to employ positive and deliberate movements to minimise fatigue and maintain tightness.
- **Step Ten:** The bar should sit dead still on the chest, but do not allow the bar to sink into the chest's musculature. This is a warning sign that you are probably losing the very important arch or bridge position. Flattening out and losing your arch will negatively affect your ability to press the bar upward. The bar should be placed roughly on the sternum, but this position can vary depending on your own individual anthropometry.
- **Step Eleven:** While pressing the bar upward, you must keep the lats fully engaged while preventing the elbows from flaring and kicking outward. If not, then you are essentially creating instability in the Glenohumeral joint, which means that the body will want to counteract by recruiting from the triceps prematurely when they are not in the most mechanically advantageous position.

19.3 The Deadlift

It goes without saying that the proper form and technique when executing the deadlift is essential to prevent injury as well as winning a competition. Judges are more likely to award you the lift if you are exhibiting proper form. Again, as with all max effort lifting, a strong tight position is key if you want to achieve the best possible 1RM.

- **Step One:** Begin by executing a few counter-movement jumps. Judge your natural power position based on where the feet land. Then, you will normally place both feet approximately half an inch closer together. A slightly narrower stance will allow for a narrower grip on the bar which will help accommodate a tighter upper back position and reduce the range of movement the bar has to travel. Place the feet at an approximate 10–15 degree angle outward.
- **Step Two:** Personally, I always recommend using a hooked grip for a number of reasons. Firstly, you are less likely to unintentionally perform with asymmetrical imbalances because there will not be any rotation of the bar created by the hand and arm differences. Secondly, the hooked grip allows for a tighter and stronger upper back position, partially due to the higher start position that it creates because the bar sits lower in the hand. Also, your scapular remains more symmetrical, allowing a tighter back position, as well. Lastly, I have never heard of anyone that has ruptured their bicep tendon while performing the hooked grip. Believe me! It takes a very long time to recover fully from any sort of lifting injury. An injury can side-line your entire powerlifting career for an indefinite amount of time.
- **Step Three:** The width of your hand grip on the bar should be as narrow and as comfortable as possible, but not so narrow that it negatively affects your leg mechanics or leg drive.
- **Step Four:** Most coaches expect you to begin with a bar placement of about mid-foot. One reason is that this position gives you a reference point to always pull from, so your training strategy is easily repeatable. Secondly, a mid-foot position allows you to find the ideal pelvis height to start your lift. This position will give you the best of both worlds. It minimises the movement arm by keeping the weight close, yet the mid-foot starting position still allows for the optimal position from the bar to provide effective leg drive.
- **Step Five:** Now bend forward towards the bar with only a small bend from the knee. Once you are holding the bar, start to bend the knees and lower the pelvis until the front of your shins are pressing against the bar. Make sure that at no point the bar rolls forward or moves in any way, or you will have to begin again to re-locate the optimal starting position for the lift.
- **Step Six:** Next, it is time to lift the rib cage upward, squeezing on the bar while pulling yourself into the tightest possible position, feeling the full extension of your spine. Caution, do not begin to lift the bar until you are in the strongest and tightest position possible, with your shoulders in-line or over the bar.
- **Step Seven:** While pulling yourself into the strongest and tightest position possible, it is important to maintain a neutral head position, looking about 3–4 feet in front of you.

- **Step Eight:** Never yank the bar off the floor, or you will lose that strong and tight position that you have been working so hard to achieve. Instead, always squeeze the bar off the floor while dragging it up the front of your legs. The bar should stay in constant contact with the legs all the way upward. Image pushing the floor away from you.
- **Step Nine:** The moment that the bar reaches the knees, aggressively drive the hips forward into the bar. If this is done correctly, then your upper legs will never lose contact with the bar.
- **Step Ten:** Always make sure to lock-out at the finish of each rep. Another good bit of advice that I always tell my lifters just before a competition lift is to always re-set between each rep and treat each rep as if it were a max single.
- **Step Eleven:** This might sound a bit obvious, but at the end of the lift, you should return the bar to the floor by simply shoving the hips backward and bending from the knees to maintain proper spinal positioning, the same as before. The bar should stay as close to the legs as possible until the bar hits the floor and remember – never let go of the bar on the way down!

20

General Information for Success

Technique, Genetics, and the 1RM Method

The simple truth about nearly all elite-level powerlifter is that they are usually blessed with either a combination of incredible genetics and good technique or incredible technique and good genetics.

This is not to say that these athletes never lift with bad technique that simply looks terribly ugly when trying to achieve a weight that no other human being on the planet could ever successfully lift. However, at the very least, athletes at this level always **train** at their best possible technical ability and are always *trying* to maintain the best possible form under incredible loads, even if it gets a bit ugly.

I have coached lots of great lifters in my career. Some have great genetics, some of them do not, but all of the truly successful powerlifters possess an impressive commitment to near-perfect technique. It is because they exhibit better technique than their competitors, that elite-level lifters tend to get three white lights and go nine-for-nine, while achieving big totals and winning numerous championships.

I have coached all levels of lifters from the very genetically gifted, to the not so genetically gifted, using the 1RM Method. Many of these same not so gifted athletes regularly beat the much stronger lifters who clearly have better genetics in competition. In fact, coaching lifters to overcome limiting factors is pretty much the basis of my career. The reason I can coach weaker, less genetically gifted lifters to win and beat naturally stronger lifters with better genetics is really very simple. **Better competition strategy! Better peaking! Better technique!** If you have all these three qualities, then you will triumph over any genetically gifted competitor who does not have all three of them!

As I consistently stress throughout this book, *Technique is King*. Lifting maximal weights is all about technique. Better lifting mechanics ultimately lead to greater loads being lifted. Here is a very simple example. Two construction workers, one with great genetics and is very strong and one with average genetics who is considerably weaker. They both have the same job, which is to loosen a few old and rusty bolts. The first genetically gifted construction worker does not have very good tools. He only has a short wrench and even with his superior strength, he is still unable to generate enough torque to loosen all the bolts. Meanwhile, the second, less genetically gifted construction worker has the proper tools for the job, a longer wrench. Even though he is as not as physically strong as the first, he is able to loosen all the bolts successfully. What would happen if you, as a competitive powerlifter, possessed all the right tools for *YOUR* job? In powerlifting, the right tools equate to better technique in all three lifts. With the right tools and better technique, any less genetically gifted lifter can easily achieve victory, time and time again.

From my experience, the example above is part of the reason that women are generally easier to coach and why they are more likely to see greater improvement in both the short- and long-term compared to their male counterparts. Women tend to choose *strategy and technique* over *brute strength*.

Another reason that *Technique is King* in competitions is because judges tend to award the lift to the lifter with better technique. Pure and simple! Like I said before, three white lights and nine-out-of-nine will always build bigger totals, and totals win championships!

Successfully lifting a 1RM relies heavily on trying to teach ideal, individual mechanics on each lift. Any coach that tells you otherwise is a complete idiot and does not understand basic biomechanics of how to best manipulate your anthropometry to better promote both short and long-term strength development.

Basic physiology proves that when golgi tendon organs and muscle spindles (proprioceptive sensory receptor organs located at the origin and insertion of skeletal muscle fibres, leading into the tendons of skeletal muscle) sense danger due to excessive loads (the danger being excessive tension or stretch), they will send information via sensory neurons to the central nervous system. The brain will then send inhibitory signals back to the prime movers, effectively turning down or shutting off the prime movers required to lift the heavy load. This is an involuntary protective mechanism. Subsequently, lifters who have better technique and therefore, lifting mechanics, will be in a better position to recruit from prime movers involved in the lift and will have less force per kg or lbs being transferred through these sensory organs. As a result, they will be better able to maintain full recruitment of the main muscle groups involved in lifting the new maximal load and will have a better greater chance of successfully completing the lift. This evidence alone lays to rest the foolish idea that powerlifting is solely about the weight lifted and that technique is irrelevant!

Do not be put off by all the talk of genetics. Remember, 'TECHNIQUE IS KING!'
You will find that almost any dedicated powerlifter can win lots of championships if they possess high levels of both technique and intelligence.

I purposely did not mention intelligence when previously describing the combination of factors that elite-level lifters need to succeed. This is simply because, most the time, the coaches behind the scenes are the ones working out all the strategies, numbers and attempt selections for the lifters. However, this is not to say these lifters are not intelligent because we have everything from surgeons to scientists on the UK team.

When coaching at the highest level in this sport, I like to think of the elite-level lifters that I am coaching as warriors who are 110% in the moment, waiting to go to war and always focusing on what needs to be done to win the battle and ultimately, the war. As an elite-level coach, it is my job to strategize and facilitate, allowing the lifters to avoid distraction while giving each lifter on the team the best possible opportunity to win or simply perform at their highest possible level.

As a lifter, you should always be striving to improve your maximal strength levels, regardless of your perceived genetics. Always striving to improve your technique on each lift and better educate yourself on all aspects of powerlifting strategies will always provide enormous results in the long run. If you want to improve your chances of winning championships, consider possibly hiring a good and reputable powerlifting coach who primarily focuses on helping to improve your lifting mechanics and teaching you great strategies for winning competitions.

What to look for when trying to find a good lifting coach

The very best coaches can always be easily identified as those whose lifters have the best form and technique. These lifters subsequently, are almost always the ones who generally have the best long-term gains and the best chance of competing at the elite-level.

Meanwhile, bad coaches can always be easily identified as they normally try to re-coach the key movements on the all-important competition day – big mistake. Their lifters generally have the worst form and technique. Some of these coaches might be fortunate enough to have one very capable and strong lifter in their charge, but in many cases, the strength of that lifter is usually due to pure genetics rather than good coaching skills. You will usually find that these types of coaches tend to only have one or two very strong lifters to their name. When you look at their overall coaching career however, they have inadvertently held back many of their lifters from achieving the highest levels of success.

Bad coaching is part of the reason for my creation of the List of **UK Best International Powerlifting Coaches**, please visit www.strengthcoachfarncombe.com. One of the many criteria that qualifies a coach to be placed on this list is being able to demonstrate a proven track record of quality lifters who have risen through the ranks to the highest level in the sport. Do not be fooled by one-hit-wonders.

You should also be aware that the very best coaches consecutively produce lifters who have the best technique. The best coaches know that without excellent lifting mechanics, our coaching efforts will be in vain. So we do not want to waste our time.

20.1 Nutrition Tips for Achieving the Best Possible 1RM

This nutrition tip may sound very simple, but when utilised effectively and properly, it can be your secret weapon on championship days.

I always recommend that lifters drink a cup of strong coffee before training on a max effort day. First, you will want to reduce your caffeine intake during the phase preceding your start of the 1RM Method. Once you begin, then you should try to consume only one cup of strong coffee before a max effort session. Then once again, you will cut out the caffeine completely in the last few days before the championships. This process will make you more caffeine-sensitive, which is exactly what you want if you want to get that extra burst of energy that you will really need on competition day.

Even though there is conflicting research on caffeine and improved strength, everyone already knows that caffeine helps to positively improve mental focus. In my experience from working with literally hundreds of athletes using only legal and sensible amounts of caffeine in this manner, I consistently witness a slight burst of improved strength and power on competition day.

This is what I recommend: **one strong cup of coffee approximately 15–20 mins before the squat event, and one or two more cups of strong coffee throughout the day, as needed.**

Remember, it will only be possible to achieve a positive effect from caffeine if you have become more caffeine-sensitive by reducing your intake beforehand.

Powerlifting is not the prettiest sport. The true champions are not always the most ripped or have the best haircuts. A true champion focuses all of their efforts on what will win competitions. Do not fall into the trap of "Going Hollywood".

My advice is to always film the angles that matter the most. These angles are generally the ones that make your technique look the worst, but this is what you want! Videos like these give you the best and most accurate feedback imaginable. Sure, your coach or your buddies can tell you what you are doing wrong, but something always gets lost in the translation. Be your own best judge and critique yourself.

But you might also consider asking for constructive criticism from your friends and lifting mates on YouTube and Facebook if you choose to post your videos online. This approach will not make you a social media sensation overnight, but you will become a great lifter that people actually respect and look to for advice and lifting tips. Long-term, you will end up lifting much bigger loads, avoiding plateaus and reducing chances of injury. Who knows? Maybe you *will* become a social media sensation, but for all the *right* reasons.

21

Glossary

Androgen Receptor – a form of nuclear receptor that is activated by binding either of the androgenic hormones, testosterone, or dihydrotestosterone in the cytoplasm and then translocating into the nucleus.

Anabolic – refers to the metabolic process that is characterized by molecular growth, such as the increase of muscle mass.

Bio motor abilities – There are 5 bio-motor abilities:

1. Strength
2. Endurance
3. Speed.
4. Flexibility.
5. Balance or coordination.

Cortisol – sometimes called "the stress hormone". Cortisol is a steroid hormone, known as a glucocorticoid, made in the adrenal glands and then released into the blood which transports it throughout the body.

Fast-twitch – muscles fibre (type IIA & IIB) fatigue faster but are used in powerful bursts of movements like sprinting and lifting heavy weights.

Gene expression – The process by which information from a **gene** is used in the synthesis of a functional **gene** product. These products are often proteins, but in non-protein coding **genes** such as transfer RNA (tRNA) or small nuclear RNA (snRNA) **genes**, the product is a functional RNA.

High threshold motor units – are capable of contracting at maximal force and velocity.

Hypertrophy – muscle hypertrophy involves an increase in the size of skeletal muscle through a growth in size of its component cells.

Homeostasis – A characteristic of a system that regulates its internal environment and tends to maintain stable, relatively constant conditions.

HRV (heart rate viability) – A system of measuring your autonomic nervous system.

Inhibitory – The act of inhibiting or the state of being inhibited; something that restrains, blocks or suppresses.

Intramuscular coordination – involves the recruitment of motor units, firing rate of motor units.

Intermuscular coordination – The synchronization of muscle groups

Kinaesthetic awareness – A sensory skill that your body uses to know where it is in space.

Microcycle – Generally a block of up to 7 days.

Mesocycle – Generally referred to as a block 3–6 microcycles, but it is typically a month.

Macrocycle – The overall training period, usually representing anything from 6–12months.

Maximal strength – The greatest amount of force that a muscle or muscle groups can voluntarily produce, regardless of time.

Methodology – A system of broad principles or rules from which specific methods or procedures may be derived to interpret or solve different problems within the scope of a particular discipline.

Motor unit – Made up of a motor neuron and the skeletal muscle fibre it innervates.

Motor Pattern – Generally a movement involved in the performance of a task. A squat, a jump, and a kick are all motor patterns.

MRV – maximum recoverable volume.

Nervous system – A complex network of nerves and cells that carry messages to and from the brain and spinal cord to various parts of the body. The nervous system includes both the central nervous system and the peripheral system.

Neural adaptation – increases in strength due to short term training are the result of neural adaptations.

Neuromuscular, or neuromuscular system – consists of the muscles and the nervous system. Under the control of the brain.

Overreaching – Training beyond the body's ability to adapt in the hope that your body super compensates, achieving higher levels of performance.

Proprioceptors – Sensors that provide information about joints angle, muscle length, and muscle tension.

Post-activation potentiation – Contractile history of muscle directly affects subsequent ability to generate force.

Potentiation – The increase in strength of nerve impulses along pathways which have been used previously, either short-term or long-term.

Parasympathetic nervous system (PNS) – One of three divisions of the autonomic nervous system. Sometimes called the rest and digest system, the parasympathetic system conserves energy as it slows the heart rate, increases intestinal and gland activity, amongst many other functions including promoting recovery.

Realisation – A realisation phase is the final stage of training before a championship. A Realisation phase starts out like a more intense form of transmutation phase, but with lower volume and higher intensities allows for more recovery between sessions. The training is directed to mainly competition lifts.

RPE (rate of perceived exertion) – training by feel.

Super compensate – The post training period during which the trained function/parameter has a higher performance capacity than it did prior to the training period.

Slow-twitch muscles fibre (type I) – Helps enable long-endurance feats such as distance running, and are not ideal for lifting large loads.

SAID – specific adaption to imposed demands.

Sympathetic nervous system (SNS) – A part of the autonomic nervous system (ANS). The sympathetic nervous system activates what is often termed the" fight or flight" response, stimulating you to lift heavy loads.

SRA – stimulus recovery adaptations.

Training age – The number of years that an athlete has specialised in a particular sport.

Training frequency – The amount of training sessions performed within a week.

Training volume is a measure of total reps per exercise, in total amount of sets per training session; in total amount of weight lifted in exercise per training session; in total amount of sets or reps per day, per week, or per year etc.

TUT – Time under tension

Transmutation – A transmutation phase is all about taking general abilities and transferring them to specific abilities. Generally high intensities and moderate volume, focussing on mainly specific/competition lifts. With some contribution of general specific lifts that build the competition movements. The goal of this block is to develop the abilities that are specific for the competition lifts, percentages of 75–90% being the norm.

Symbols and Abbreviations

1RM – Single Maximal Effort

SPP – Specific Preparation Phase

GPP – General Preparation Phase

Hyp – Hypertrophy

HIFI – High Frequency High Intensity

People I Would Like to Thank Personally

22

Acknowledgments

Charles Poliquin

Thanks to Charles Poliquin for helping me to put all pieces together as an S&C coach. I had been an S&C coach for nearly ten years before studying under Charles. By studying his coaching principles and through his guidance, I have achieved phenomenal success with athletes from many sports.

Arun Singh

Thanks to Arun Singh for supporting my role as the UK Head Classic Powerlifting Coach and for essentially being more of a mentor to me. Arun has taught so much regarding international-level powerlifting. With all the respect that I can muster, I call Arun *the Oracle,* because in Great Britain he is the man who knows anything and everything you will ever need to know about coaching lifters at International Level Championships. Furthermore, he has always been only a phone call away whenever I need anything.

SBD Ben Banks

Ben is a phenomenal coach with an incredible knowledge of international powerlifting. Ben was one of coaches to really make me question the extrinsic mechanics of each lift. Ben made me question our ability to learn or re-learn movements. Out of many of these conversations was born my three phase system, which allows lifters to finally achieve their best possible lifting mechanics on each lift to better suit their own anthropometry.

Eric Cressey

I was lucky enough to spend a very short amount of time with Eric, who helped formulate a program for one of my lifters. Eric was incredibly helpful in discussing thoroughly and systematically every aspect of his program design principles. His work has been a great learning tool for me as a professional coach and has influenced my coaching style to this very day. Eric is also an incredibly competitive powerlifter himself and is always a great source of information.

Louie Simmons

I've never met Mr. Simmons, but without him, I can't imagine what the current state of competitive powerlifting would be. He is such an incredible wealth information.

Paul Rees

Paul has consecutively produced many great lifters for such a long time. I remember Paul coaching when I was lifting. I'm not sure if Paul knows this, but he was one of the coaches who inspired me to start coaching. Paul is a thoroughly down to Earth and approachable gentleman, as well as a great coach; one of UK's finest.

Dean Bowring

Dean has also inspired me into coaching optimal lifting mechanics. Most of the fundamental extrinsic mechanics I coach to this day came from watching Dean lift. I would then go away and deconstruct all the extrinsic mechanics of his lifts to thoroughly understand how he could lift such incredible loads. Dean is not just a great lifter, he is also a great coach of whom I cannot speak highly enough.

Mark Giles

Mark, for being a great coach and helping create order in the Great Britain Classic Powerlifting team. Mark has set an incredibly high standard to try and live up to, a standard towards which I am still aiming.

GB Coach Pete Sparks

Pete has played an integral role in supporting the GB team achieve such incredible results.

Like myself, Pete works long hours and yet still finds time to work with the team. He helps not just on the platform, but for months in advance of Championships. He works tirelessly and commits fully to getting the best possible results for Great Britain.

Finally, I would like to thank the greats

- Y Verkhoshansky
- A.S.Medvedyev
- V Zatzorsky
- Mel Siff

Without these guys, we would all be *pissing in the wind and calling it rain.*

Let's be honest, without the incredible individuals listed above, we would still be in the dark without a clue for how to design effective methodologies for improving maximal strength. I remember back in the early 1990's, the only research and numerous publications out there seemed to all be outlining different methods for increasing performance in the cardiovascular system. There was very little *good* information in the UK on strength training and how to improve the neuromuscular system.

The only information that you could find at the time was by reading some very old books written by old school strongmen dating as far back as the 1800–1900's. Reading these books was great, but trying to find them was like a needle in the proverbial haystack. They essentially lacked any substantive research or adequate explanations of strength gains.

Then in the 1980's and certainly throughout the early 1990s, bodybuilding became the next big fad to hit the UK (and from what I understand, most of the west). However, once again, all of the documented bodybuilding protocols were essentially based on bullshit. They were books written by "authors" who were simply trying to make a quick buck! They were trying to sell a crap system or some crap supplement (that usually tasted horrid) that never provided any real, visible, measurable results with regards to strength development. It is really shameful that all the best information lay hidden behind the Berlin Wall for nearly

60-years and that it has taken such a considerably long time for this information to filter out, even after the fall of the Berlin Wall in 1989.

Remember, the Internet did not really kick off until the mid 1990's and it took even longer before any good information about strength development began appearing online.

I really hope you can take the information in this book and use it to start experiencing the benefits of better quality lifting in your training and competitions, but more importantly, consistently and effectively build on your true 1RM.

For further information please check out www.strengthcoachfarncombe.com

Instagram: @strengthcoachfarncombe

Facebook: Strength Coach Farncombe

Twitter: @UKstrengthcoach

9 781786 230355